Pathways
of
Chance

F. David Peat

Pathways
of
Chance

Pari
Publishing

"Here we have that rare and wonderful thing: a scientist who can truly write. Peat's autobiography is a daring fusion of the memoir and the cutting-edge essay. It makes a rich and readable introduction, not only to Peat's own extraordinary life and his web of 20th-century connections, but also to some of the most tantalizing ideas and figures of the period, across both science and art. It is, at times, provocative; at other times, poignantly human. Throughout, it is erudite and, above all, keenly concerned about how we, as a species and a planet, move forward in the 21st-century. Peat's words are subtle catalysts, sparking in us our own potential for transformation at all levels of life. *Pathways of Chance* is a fascinating book, and an important one. Read it now."
~**Alison MacLeod**, author of *The Wave Theory of Angels* and *Fifteen Modern Tales of Attraction*

"David Peat has one of the liveliest, most wide-ranging, depth-probing minds I've ever encountered. Peat's thoughts on physics, philosophy and the arts, put forward in a genial, gracious writing style read like a can't-put-down mystery novel. *Pathways of Chance* will surely appeal to all who are interested in any of these subjects as well as those who like reading about his and other famous people's fascinating lives."
~**Joseph Eger**, Conductor, Symphony for United Nations and author of *Einstein's Violin: A Conductor's Notes on Music, Physics and Social Change*

"...a delightful and informative read."
~**David Lorimer**, *Network Review: Journal of the Scientific and Medical Network*

"...a physicist committed to a radical vision of life...His own life, presented in this engaging spiritual journey, is a persuasive illustration of that much-needed change [of society]."
~**Chris Clarke**, *Resurgence*

Book design and cover by Andrea Barbieri
Printed and bound in Italy by Grafiche Vieri, Roccastrada (GR)
Printed on 100% chlorine-free recycled paper

Pari Publishing

Via Tozzi 7, 58040 Pari, Grosseto, Italy
www.paripublishing.com

For Chiara

TABLE OF CONTENTS

ACKNOWLEDGEMENTS

The author would like to thank the following for their support
and encouragement both in the writing of this book
and in the creation of Pari Publishing:
Andrea Barbieri, Santi di Renzo, Maureen Doolan,
Mary Flanagan, David Godwin, Margaret Harrell,
Donald Liebich, Alison MacLeod, Therese Schroeder-Sheker,
Eleanor F. Peat, Kim Williams.

F. David Peat

Pathways
of Chance

Publishing

Introduction

People make their journeys in different ways. Some discuss their plans with a travel agent several months in advance. They scan the Internet to gather information on their destination. They look for the best beach, choose a hotel, note temperatures, search for nightspots and check out the restaurants and shopping. For such people a vacation goes as smoothly as possible when there are no surprises. Everything has been preplanned. Like the Duc Des Esseintes in J.-K. Huysman's *A Rebours*, they have already taken their vacation mentally before leaving home

On the other hand, there are those who will get into a rental car at the airport without having the slightest idea of where they will be spending the night. They drive and explore possibilities. If a lake, seashore or small town looks attractive they stop for a day or two. Only when they reach a crossroads, do they decide whether to turn left or right.

I'm the latter type of traveler. I enjoy surprises. I'm always open for the unexpected to turn up. All this is by way of introducing a metaphor about life. Just as with a vacation, there are some who in their mid twenties have already planned every step of their lives. Their career path has been determined and they have clear ideas about retirement. Sometimes fate plays tricks on these best-laid plans, yet when I look back at some of my friends from school or university I can't help noticing that in so many cases their lives have proceeded along the plans they laid down when we talked long into the night about what we would do in the future.

Much depends on how we react when the unexpected occurs and a new door temporarily opens. Do we compensate as best we can and attempt to remain on our predetermined track or do we ask, "What is life trying to say to me? In what direction could this new possibility take me? Is it worth suspending what I am doing at the moment in order to explore something new?"

What if we leave room in our lives for chance and the unexpected? It means that the future is less predictable. Instead of seeing one's life planned out into the future like a vast highway, life only makes sense to us when we look back to the past and see the path we have taken with all its diversions, U-turns and side roads. There may have been no fixed plan for the future but looking back at that map of a life's journey it almost seems as if there had indeed been a goal all along, but a goal that had been concealed at every step of the way.

This little autobiography is about looking back and trying to read the pattern of a life. It asks why a person born in Liverpool, England with a passion for science should have found himself sitting in a tepee talking with Native Americans or living in a medieval Italian village. It asks why a person who had devoted his life to exploring ideas and abstractions should end up talking about such things as ethics or gentle action. It is also a book about intellectual explorations. For this reason following each autobiographical chapter there is an "excursion," an essay that explores in greater depth one of the scientific or philosophical themes that has come to fascinate me.

GROWING UP IN LIVERPOOL

Chapter 1

I was born in 1938, just before the outbreak of World War II. The location was Waterloo, a suburb of Liverpool, Britain's major seaport for trade with the Americas. Part of my early childhood was spent being woken in the middle of the night and carried into a damp and smelly air raid shelter. Two persistent dreams remained from that period and continued until the middle of my life. One was of looking up into the night sky. Suddenly the stars begin to move and I experience a shifting of my axis. It was only in 1971, during a power strike in London when the city was plunged into darkness, that I saw, within a dark sky, the lights of aircraft bound for Heathrow and Gatwick airports. It was then that I realized my recurring dream involved an early wartime memory of searchlights and tracer bullets in the sky.

Another dream is about a forgotten crime revealed by the digging up of a dead body. What Freudian meaning could this contain? In the dream, and almost at the moment of waking, I was clothed in the sense that I must have done something truly terrible in the past, something so dark that it had been repressed from my consciousness.

This time the historical origins of the dream revealed itself shortly before my mother died. It also dated back to the war days, a time of stringent rationing. Somehow my father had obtained a Christmas turkey, no doubt on the black market. But by Christmas Eve the bird had begun to stink. As my mother related this incident, memories suddenly flooded back—a whispered conversation in the kitchen. How could they dispose of the carcass that my grandmother jokingly referred to as "the body"? At that time government snoopers examined the contents of garbage cans and there was a heavy fine for people who threw away food, maybe even imprisonment for those dealing on the black market. So when it was dark my father went into the garden, dug a hole and "buried the body," with jokes about people digging it up in the future. I remember my fear that somehow the crime would be revealed and my father would be arrested and taken away.

Two dreams and two interpretations that refer to real, traumatic events in the past yet these dreams are also doors into something darker and deeper. Needless to say, after the actual historical correspondences had been revealed the repeated occurrence of the dreams vanished.

Waterloo, where I grew up, was a suburb of Liverpool but my grandmother, who was born in the 1870s, remembered it as a village surrounded by fields and farms. The local doctor made his rounds in his horse and trap. The vicar arrived at the church on horseback. I was close to my grandmother who took me on walks so that I could watch the blacksmith near the Liver Hotel putting the shoes on horses. This, she told me, was once a coaching stop and she remembered the coaches traveling north to the Lake District across the Preston sands at low tide.

My mother and father sometimes took me to the end of the bus route and from there we would walk to the Sniggery Woods or through the village of Little Crosby. Around us was the rich and fertile Lancashire plain with its fields of wheat and potatoes. The village of Little Crosby itself had escaped the Protestant Reformation. There were stories of priests being smuggled across from Ireland, and of a continuity of religious ceremonies held in that tiny village that dated back before Henry VIII.

But that bucolic life was far from my own. The place where we lived was as rich in class gradations as to make the Indian caste system appear simplistic. The other side of Queensway, the street on which I lived, lay in Crosby which was a far "nicer" place to live, and so the houses were more expensive. We, however, lived on the side that belonged to Waterloo that was somewhat down-market. Indeed as one moved from street to street—a distance of only a few hundred yards—accents and jobs changed in a clearly discernable way.

My father was an electrician who over the years bettered him-self, moving from the strong Labour Party background of his family to the Conservative Party and eventually to become Town Mayor. My mother, for her part, attempted to "talk posh" and put on a special sort of artificial accent when visitors came. My mother had once been a piano teacher and my early memories are of being placed in a chair while she played Chopin or Men-delssohn's "Songs without Words." Sometimes my father would stand at her side and sing songs popularized by Fred Astaire. (My mother suspected a smoldering passion for Ginger Rogers in this.)

During the war my father, as an electrician, was in what was termed a reserved occupation. For a time he was away setting up an American hospital in Hereford, then back in Liverpool doing other work deemed essential to the war effort. If he wasn't in the army then at least he was in "Dad's Army"—the Home Guard. Once, during an exercise, he fell over a wall and broke his little finger. At the end of the war he received a medal and citation from the King—sent to all those who had risked their lives and been wounded in the defense of their country!

There was one occasion in which he indeed was sent to defend the nation. Neighbors believed they had seen a parachute de-scend on some waste land and came to our door demanding that my father scour the surrounding fields to apprehend the "Ger-man spy." My father fetched his rifle, which he kept on top of the wardrobe. He couldn't however find any bullets because my mother, who lived in constant fear, had hidden them. A great argument followed, with neighbors waiting at the front door. Finally my mother handed him some bullets. He was gone for a long time but returned saying he had found nothing. Who knows–the neighbors could have been mistaken. Or possibly my father and the spy arrived at some type of mutual agreement of non-interference in each other's business.

Seen in retrospect my father must have been a frustrated man. He attempted to better himself with study at night so that he could gain qualifications to become an illuminating engineer. From there he joined Blackler's, a department store in the center of Liverpool, where he rose to be Maintenance Manager. Yet with a wife who would not accompany him to dinners or on excursions he became increasingly irritable. He was also annoyed at the attention directed towards her son, myself. More and more there were outbursts of anger, which frightened me as a child. Once my mother attempted to run away, and when he screwed shut the front door so she couldn't escape, she pushed me out of the front room window and together we ran to the bus stop and went to stay with my aunt for a few days.

My grandmother had moved in to help my mother when I was born, and there she remained for the next thirty years or so until her death. Later, on the death of her husband, when I was around twelve, my aunt moved to a house a few doors away and so my home was a place of whispers, of meetings behind closed doors, of mysteries and matters designed to exclude my father. Maybe it was this atmosphere of secrets and occult signals that first aroused my interest in mysteries and ambiguities. The English novelist, Beryl Bainbridge, told me that her own taste for writing had its origins in the mystery that revolved around her father and the documents she had to sign as a child. Only later did she realize he was an undischarged bankrupt. Such an environment of clues and mysteries drove her to become one of England's leading writers. In my case I think it directed me to science, as a way of uncovering clues to the mysteries that surround all of us.

In this house of whispers my grandmother was a tower of strength. She was an immensely practical woman. As a widow she had brought up her two daughters alone. Or at least that's what I was led to believe until another round of whispers began in my early teens. It turned out that my grandfather had been alive all the time and had only recently died. He had been thrown out of the house because of a tendency to gamble and my grandmother had forged on alone.

In order to survive she had taken in washing and continued to work even with a high fever that turned into pneumonia. She told me how she had to have an operation to drain a lung but without an anesthetic for, as the operation began, the anesthesiologist said, "The heart, she is embarrassed." There was indeed a weakness in her heart. I recall a time when she had been confined to bed for several days and a specialist had been brought in. After examining her he spoke to my mother and aunt downstairs. He said that the main artery was severely restricted and she would remain in bed for the rest of her life–which would not be for too long. As he left and the door closed behind him my grandmother came downstairs. "I've decided to get up," she said. "I've been in bed too long and there's the kitchen to clean." All protests were in vain. Once I asked her if she was afraid of death. "I'll go when God calls me, and not before," was her reply. She must have lived on a good twenty years after that specialist's visit.

Her education had been at what was called a "dame school"–a school run by one woman for children of all ages. She had absorbed all she had been taught by rote–history, geography, poetry and mnemonic rhymes–far more than any child would be expected to memorize and retain today. She was also a source of old sayings–some of which probably went back to Shakespeare's day. She remembered the bells ringing at the Relief of Mafeking. She told me of her nephew who had joined the army during the

1914-18 war by pretending he was 18 when in fact he was much younger. He had refused the bottle of brandy handed around before going over the top to cross no man's land, and had been killed in the charge. She told me of more ancient matters, of an ancestor who had been a great healer and had left his village in order to cure the sick during the Plague of London.

I saw less of the relatives on my father's side. Mainly this was caused by my mother's disinclination to travel and her desire to keep me by her side. My great-grandfather on my father's side had been captain of *The Shooting Star*–a sailing ship that continued to trade with the southern states during the American Civil War. I even have a piece of music "The Shooting Star Gallop" dedicated to him. I remember his ceremonial sword on display in my grandparents' home. His son, my grandfather, had also gone to sea. He had been shipwrecked in the Gulf of St Lawrence and survived a long journey in an open boat.

His wife, my grandmother, came from the Lake District and had the accent of that area. Years later my father took me to see the family home, to the land of Wordsworth and the Lake Poets. I have a dim memory of dining in a small hotel and my father asking the owner about a "Secret Valley" that had featured in a popular novel about a character called Rogue Herries. The owner told my father that the author was still alive and that he could arrange a meeting. We were then admitted into Hugh Walpole's room. The old man did not seem particularly interested in my father but was keen to give me a message. He told me that I shouldn't go to the cinema or listen too much to the radio, but go for walks in the country. It did not seem to be particularly profound advice, but neither was Walpole a particularly great writer.

But I'm getting too far into the story. Let me backtrack a little. As I mentioned earlier, my first memories are of being pulled out of bed at night, wrapped in a blanket, and taken to the air raid shelter at the bottom of the garden. The bomb run for German aircraft was along the River Mersey towards their target–the Liverpool docks. In so doing they passed over the area where I lived. Next morning older boys would be out scouring the area for shrapnel and the magnesium casing from incendiary bombs.

There was also the dimmest memory of something approaching paradise at my aunt's house. They lived at Hunt's Cross on the other side of Liverpool. While it was not far from the city center, the bombers would by then have dropped their loads and begun their long flight back. For this reason the nights at Hunt's Cross were quiet and peaceful. There were no air raid sirens; instead I could hear the sounds of the steam trains on the line not far from the house.

My uncle had been a ship's engineer in the Merchant Navy. When war broke out he was about to be assigned to the *Ark Royal*, an aircraft carrier that was torpedoed and sunk with great loss of life. However fate had something else in store for him and he was sent to work at Hunt's Cross for The Distillers Company, which was involved in the large-scale production of penicillin.

My aunt and uncle's house was a magic island far from the tensions of war and the household in which I lived. My aunt worked as a volunteer nurse, but also had a passion for painting. My uncle's spare time was spent in his garage working with wood. As I grew a little older he would show me how to make a boat or a toothbrush stand.

It was in this house that I first learned about science. My aunt had a microscope with a collection of slides. It had a little mirror at the bottom that you had to tilt to bring in the light. I loved to look through that microscope and once when the house was deserted I took down the box, assembled the instrument and began to look at the slides. I remember my aunt's amazement when she returned and the whispering to my uncle in the kitchen as to how I had managed to set it up correctly.

All this was before I could read and write and so my aunt would turn over the pictures of a book, *The Marvels and Myster-*

ies of Science, with its photographs of the moon and planets, its cutaways of volcanoes and its drawings of the body as a little factory. My aunt would tell me the stories behind each photograph and diagram. I was particularly interested in the fact that we were made out of protons and electrons. It seemed to my mind, at the time, that we must all be made out of electricity, which was not like any concrete substance at all. I suppose that still remains something of a puzzle even today!

It was as a small boy in my aunt's house that I first experienced the physicality of a paradigm shift. I had constructed my own cosmology, put together through scraps of overheard conversation, and believed that we were literally inside the earth. The earth was a hollow ball. Inside were the sky, sun, moon and stars. One looked "up" into the sky by looking to the center of the cosmos. If one dug holes in the garden, as I did, one would go on forever outwards.

Then one night, lying in my bed and about to go to sleep my aunt make a remark which suddenly made me realize that we lived on the surface of the ball and that the sky was not inside but above. That moment my entire vision of the cosmos shifted in such a sudden and profound movement that I felt it as a physical shifting of my insides, a moment of total vertigo. I don't think that at any time since have I ever experienced a transformation in my thinking as profound. Nevertheless internal sensations of movement and transformation have always been important to me and are the subject of the first essay-diversion in this autobiography.

SENSING THE BODY

Excursion I

The French psychiatrist Jacques Lacan argued that consciousness is structured like a language. He claimed that not only is consciousness ordered in the same way as a language but also that actual words are trapped, they are literally imprisoned, within the body as psychophysical symptoms. I would go further and argue that the linguistic dimension to consciousness is part of a much larger continuing cycle that arises out of psychophysical processes occurring deep within the body, and often outside general awareness. These are then projected outward onto the external world in the form of gestures, actions, words and so on. As a further part of this whole process, the projected material can then be internalized into awareness where it is encoded or structured in ways that may well include Lacan's linguistic system of differences and trapped words. In turn, this internalized material works within the body to be projected outwards again.

By being released into the "open air," as it were, projected material is free to become active at both the social and interpersonal levels. Yet, at the same time, it is part of the one indivisible process and must at some point be internalized and returned to the body to continue through the same cycles of projection and internalization.

Psychotherapists such as Wilhelm Reich and Stanislav Grof have emphasized the notion that consciousness is not simply an activity of the brain but also has correlates within the physical body. The paragraphs above may sound very academic but the ideas I want to present here do not come from some scholarly study of psychology but out of my own experience and my many discussions with artists about the ways they work and experience their own creativity.

Artists and musicians undergo a long training to refine their skills. Most of them engage in their work with a great degree of passion. It is for these reasons that I find that their sensibilities about the consciousness of the entire body are sometimes more developed than the average. This ability to touch the deepest levels of psychophysical consciousness may explain why art and music have always been of such significance to the human race. Art and music make manifest, by bringing into conscious awareness, that which has previously been felt only tentatively and internally. Art, in its widest sense, is a form of play that lies at the origin of all making, of language, and of the mind's awareness of its place within the world. Art, in all its forms, makes manifest the spiritual dimension of the cosmos and expresses our relationship to the natural world. This may have been the original cause of that light which first illuminated the preconscious mind of early hominids.

Anish Kapoor, for example, is a sculptor of international standing whose work has been described as both mysterious and beautiful. He speaks of the generation of such work as beginning with an intentionality that lies beyond planning and thinking. This intentionality must be held within, to the point where energy builds to such intensity that the artist must then get out of the way, abdicate the self, and allow the art to emerge into the world. The extent that ego and personal biography remain is the extent to which the work fails to make its full impact. The most successful pieces, however, undergo what Kapoor describes as an alchemical transformation and have a universal presence.

The composer Sir Michael Tippett (perhaps best known for

his oratorio *A Child of Our Time*) described to me how his music contains tensions, movements, transformations, dramas, oppositions and resolutions, all of which had to be held within his physical body before the act of composition. The creative work of consciousness requires acts of suspension, containment and holding within the body, which correspond to the important Negrido state of alchemy. As with all creative work, a significant stage is the Negrido in which nothing appears to happen. The Negrido can be equated with creative depression, a tense state of holding that precedes the creative outpouring.

In such a state, characteristic of all creative work, the physical body must contain the work so that it can be "cooked" to the point where it can be expressed in words, music or art. In Tippett's case, when the Negrido state ended, his music was freed ready to be projected outward into the world and objectified as notes written on manuscript paper. As potential sound it had now entered the manifest world and at this point intellectual work, judgment, discriminations and editing were required. Yet an important, possibly the most important, phase had already taken place in those processes of consciousness that lie outside immediate mental awareness, specifically within the muscular tensions, suspended disposition to movement, metabolic flows, senses of orientation, heartbeats, and so on, of Tippett's body.

Perhaps the painter Cézanne gave the most famous example of the way internal sensations of the body become the source of art. Faced with a landscape, mountain or still life, the painter worked directly from his "little sensations," never abstracting himself from the scene, or taking things for granted, or working at second hand as did the studio painters of the nineteenth century. In his work Cézanne was always questioning, always taking a second look, always correcting.

The philosopher Merleau-Ponty wrote of "Cézanne's doubt." That is, the artist's passionate need to look again and again. Cézanne himself expressed it in the following way, "I am becoming more lucid before nature, but always with me the realization of my sensations is always painful. I cannot attain the intensity that is unfolded before my senses…. Here on the bank of the river the motifs multiply, the same subject seen from a different angle offers subject for study of the most powerful interest and so varied that I think I could occupy myself for months without changing place by turning now more to the right, now more to the left."

And this is exactly what I experience in front of a painting by Cézanne. Over the years I looked again and again at Cézanne and was never able to find a place of rest and certainty. As a result, I began to reread what art historians had written about Cézanne and tried to apply their findings to my own experiences as I stood before his canvases. All well and good, yet I felt that nothing of what I had read was really touching the essential fact of my engagement with the work. It was only a few years ago, at my own point of doubt and suspension, that I realized that I had all along been listening to the sensations within my own body, to minimal muscular movements, suspended dispositions to motion, and body orientation and disturbances to the proprioception. I noticed that those dislocations of a tabletop, the tilting of a figure, the movement of brush strokes, the conflicting orientations of planes were producing in me sensations of movement—or rather suspensions of the disposition to move. And, like a piece of music, these sensations, these embryonic movements, dispositions and emotions were all working together. At that moment I felt that Cézanne was evoking in me something of the "little sensations" he had experienced a century before. In fact Cézanne was "playing" my mind and body like a musical instrument and I was responding to what had been first produced in Cézanne as he stood before his motif. The painter had discovered a way of encoding his sensations, just as a composer like Tippett could encode, via musical notes, the sensations of an opera.

This interior work, which precedes mental awareness, is not confined to art and music alone. It is echoed in a remark the physicist David Bohm made about working in quantum theory, "I had the feeling that internally I could participate in some movement that was the analogy of the thing you are talking about. I can't really articulate it. It had to do with a sense of tensions in the body; the fact that two tensions are in opposite directions and then suddenly feel that there was something else. The spin thing cannot be reduced to classical physics. Two feelings in the mind combine to produce something that is of a different quality.... I got the feeling in my own mind of spin up, spin down, that I was spinning up and then down. Then suddenly bringing them together in the x direction (Horizontal).... It's really hard to get an analogy. It's a kind of transformation that takes place. Essentially I was trying to produce in myself an analogy of that, in my state of being. In a way I'm trying to become an analogy of that–whatever that means." Bohm also talked about his way of "thinking" to Einstein who indicated that his own mathematical "thought" took place at the level of internal muscular tensions. He would sometimes squeeze a rubber ball while thinking about the non-linear differential equations of space-time.

Musical performers appear to be involved in something similar. Evidence from brain scans, together with other investigations, suggests that performance depends upon the orchestration of internal body states of movement, balance, heartbeat and so on. Surprising as it may seem, while a person is actively playing music their brain's auditory activity is somewhat suppressed. This suggests that performance involves a response to, and an expression of, inner feelings, emotions and sensations. Once, for example, during practice of a troublesome passage, the Canadian pianist Glenn Gould turned on a radio so loudly that it drowned out his "hearing" of the music he was playing. In this way his effort became focused on externalizing, or projecting outwards, his internal sensations about the music rather than in paying attention to the resultant sound he was producing.

An artist may be working on a piece when internal sensations of movement and stillness, of tension and resolution, begin to emerge. As this external and projected manifestation starts to take on a particular form and visual language, so too the artist responds, internalizing yet again. The whole flow becomes an alchemical cycle, a constant movement between inner and outer worlds. Later the viewer of the work seeks to place his or her own sense of ontological being, of body existence, and mental coherence, into relationship with the work. Great art has a transformative effect precisely because it involves one's whole being in integrative movements not dissimilar to those first experienced by the artists themselves.

When a creator's work has finally been projected externally and expressed as a manifest form, symbol, act of speech or writing, it is objectified and freed to be internalized yet again, but this time into the conscious realm of concept and thought. In this sense one only knows what one is doing when one projects it into the outer world and, as it were, sees it new-born for the first time. Often a creator does not really know the value of a piece of work until it has been objectified, made public and thereby separated from its creative host.

The function of art is to take our experiences of the world at the individual, social, cosmic and spiritual levels and allow them to attain internal coherence. We do this by containing them within the alchemical vessel of the body-mind to the point where they can be expressed externally as the engagement of inner form with the material contingencies of the outer world. In this way the invisible is made manifest, set free and given an independent ontological existence so that it can later be consciously recognized and internalized as thought, emotions, sensations and so on. Through such processes the consciousness of the body is finally released into public symbolism, language, form, physical structures where it can be absorbed and discussed by others as ideas and concepts as well as through their feelings and emotions.

Consciousness is much wider than that which is available to

awareness. Consciousness in the widest sense is a property of the entire body—muscles, viscera, metabolism and brain. This means that a great deal of our creative lives takes place outside immediate awareness. What people normally mean by "consciousness" is something structured by the ego and containing a "self" that appears to direct thought and makes decisions and so on. But such self-awareness, at best, is only a fleeting thing. We sense a succession of mental events but they are only tiny icebergs floating upon a much greater ocean of general consciousness.

Our sense of reality, and of our self as the begetter of action, is made up of a series of temporary moments of awareness. These are conjured together to produce the illusion of continuity. Awareness is like watching a movie—a series of static shots interspersed by darkness that the brain patches over to produce the illusion of continuous reality.

Our normal ego requires such illusions. It demands a sense of continuity, even to the extent of manufacturing the mental illusions that sustain this very sense. We lead much of our lives asleep and manufacture all manner of excuses to allow our dreams to continue. We believe we are living in the light of awareness, making conscious plans and decisions, but the ego is a great fabricator. Much of our true creative lives takes place outside awareness while that of which we are aware—neurotic symptoms, solving crossword puzzles, and doing routine calculations—is in fact the most superficial.

IDEAS AND REFLECTIONS

Chapter 2

In addition to *The Marvels and Mysteries of Science*, my aunt had a collection of books bound in red leather called The *Universal Home Encyclopedia*. These didn't have any pictures but I still wanted to know what was in them and so my aunt related to me her own version of the Greek philosophers. In the afternoon, when she took a rest, we would discuss Plato, the notion of forms, and the running of an ideal society.

Her education at school had probably ended at the age of fifteen or sixteen. Everything else had been picked up via the newspapers, radio and these home encyclopedias. At all events she set me thinking about the nature of the universe. I became interested in the world of matter. The world directly available to my senses differed from the interior world of my thoughts and the world of spirit. The world of spirit was very real to me then, maybe I was in that Wordsworthian state of "trailing clouds of glory" and believed that I had come from somewhere else that had been in a certain sense perfect. (Or maybe it was my own projection derived from Freud's oceanic feeling of the earliest stage of infancy.) For a time, I became preoccupied with the nature of the outer material world and with the problem of evil. This was also wartime. Fathers went away never to come back. Bombs fell near our house and we were forced to spend hours in a rank, damp air raid shelter. Why did all this happen in the world? And so I would rattle on to my aunt about "the problem of evil" while she did the dishes or applied Wallpamure (a wartime paint substitute) to the walls.

It was now time for primary school of which I have only the dimmest memories. But one thing sticks out in my mind; these were the large hard-backed notebooks my uncle gave me. One of these was to serve as a Grand Encyclopedia in which I glued diagrams and short articles gleaned from newspapers and the *Radio Times*. In another I began the cartoon adventures of Mr. Potts who traveled in a rocket and encountered Martians. In yet another I began to write stories. These were long episodic adventures that I was then allowed to relate to the class during one of the school periods. I suppose it gave the teachers a rest and diverted the other students. At times I would work myself into a corner, such as the incident of the hero who was under mortal attack in the jungle while his feet were trapped in a man-eating plant. I told my teacher that I was unable to continue his story that day–but he hinted at a way out. "Jim loosened the laces of his shoes and with one bound leapt for the branch above." Of course I didn't realize at that time I would end up writing books for a living–or correction, "for a minimal living."

As for my passion for science? I think that began back in my aunt's house with the microscope and that *Marvels and Mysteries of Science*. The idea of science suggested to me there could be an area of certainty in an uncertain world. Science told us about how things worked. It showed the way things fitted together. It was about certainty, about what could be said for sure about the world. It offered explanations. It contained principles capable of integrating together many different things. I understood this at a very early age–the way so many diverse phenomena and experiences could be gathered under the umbrella of science.

But this was not science in the abstract. It was something entirely tangible to me. One Christmas–I must have been around ten at the time–I was given a chemistry set and pretty soon devoted all my time to doing experiments. After I had left primary school and entered grammar school I struck up a friendship with the man in the local chemist's shop and would talk to him about the experiments I needed to do, but which required a supply of more advanced chemicals—fuming nitric acid, iodine crystals, potassium chlorate, and so on. He was sympathetic and supplied me with all I needed. Soon I was busy creating gases, dissolving things, making crystals, passing electrical currents through solutions.

At first my experiments were done in the kitchen. I would take the copper shielding from batteries, dissolve it in acid to produce a beautiful clear blue liquid and then leave it to stand and watch small crystals form. Chemistry allowed me to transform matter into its various forms, solids, liquids and gases, to combine them together again and then separate them into other components. These chemicals and elements had individual personalities for me and I was probably close in spirit to an alchemist of old. I no longer do experiments today but the spirit remains and has been transferred to cooking—another advantage of living in Italy.

As time progressed, my experiments became unacceptable to the family. I dissolved part of the interior of our refrigerator. I managed to ignite the magnesium casing of an incendiary bomb, which threatened to burn its way through the kitchen floor. The last straw was my experiments on polymerization involving formaldehyde and other chemicals whose names I can no longer recall. The reaction occurred in the gas phase, filling the house with dense evil-smelling smoke and fine particles that took several days to clean up. After that I was forced to transfer my laboratory to the coal shed.

One afternoon, after working in the coal shed, I believed I had made nitroglycerine—a high explosive that detonates when shaken or dropped. I retreated to my bedroom with the hope that my father wouldn't need to get extra coal that night. On another occasion I was doing some bizarre experiment in my bedroom involving passing electricity through various solutions. Needing even more electrical power I bypassed the fuse box in our house and, as a result, blacked out a number of neighboring streets.

My other passion was reading. Although I only had a junior ticket at our local library I pleaded with the librarian to allow me into the adult section upstairs so that I could borrow science books. I even had a plan to start writing science books of my own. I worked through such books as Bertrand Russell's *ABC of Relativity*, and James Jeans' *The Mysterious Universe*. Once, during a physics lesson at school, I was caught with a book under my desk. I recall the teacher creeping up behind me and grabbing the book out of my hand. "Ah Peat, if you spent as much time attending to your lessons as you do to reading books by…er…Einstein? Can you really understand this?"

Only part of the time was spent in the coal shed because I was a sickly child. There was a high degree of neurosis in the home and my mother, being a professional invalid, would often keep me at home because of suspected illnesses. My mother's addiction to illness of all forms probably originated when she was confined to a sanitarium as a girl because of tuberculosis. I, too, was in and out of hospital for minor operations and once, for several weeks I was kept home. This may well have been because they suspected that I had "a touch of TB." This disease was only spoken of in whispers since tuberculosis was associated with poverty.

Being in bed meant being off school for long periods of time and so I could read as many books as I wanted. When I got bored I traveled in my imagination, played with soldiers, or my toy farm. I rigged up a pulley system in my bedroom so that I could transport toys up to the curtain rail and back. Hour after hour, day after day, I would lie in bed, listening to the sounds of children playing outside, watching the shadows move across the bedroom ceiling and the light fade.

I was a solitary child who lived much in the imagination. I did, however, get on very well with adults. I also had a group of younger children whom I organized into playing the Olympic games. It was around this age I stood under a street lamp and wondered if the light went on forever and ever and ever. If it ever did reach the end of the universe how would it travel? When it reached the end would it simply go on traveling and making more and more space to move in?

It was around this period that I saw my uncle for the last time. It was significant because I had just gone into long pants from the short trousers I had up to now worn all my life. Uncle Tim drove the family to the seaside town of Southport for the afternoon. He was a careful driver but on the way back made two mistakes and seemed preoccupied. That night he was rushed to hospital with a perforated appendix. He wrote to me from hospital and I sent him a letter with some drawings. After a day or two peritonitis set in and he developed a high fever. Later my aunt told me he kept calling out to see the little letter I had written. The following day my mother came into my bedroom to tell me my uncle had died. It was a great blow to me.

My secondary school was certainly not one of the best but I struck up a friendship with some other boys interested in science. In many ways the teachers seemed to be out of a film by Fellini. A mathematics master who had taken to drink was bathed in cynicism. He had once taught at a fine public school but now staggered in of a morning with pieces of sticking plaster on his forehead. Another master had a memory so clouded that many years later, on seeing me in the street in my early twenties, asked why I wasn't at school. The woodwork teacher kept control by flinging pieces of wood at unruly students. There was an assistant chemistry teacher who periodically wept when he recalled the death of Scott of the Antarctic. This was tied up in some mysterious way with the fact that Scott ran out of fuel because at low temperatures the sealing on his fuel cans had turned into some other allotropic form of the metal and so leaked. Was he crying for the death of Scott or for Scott's ignorance of basic chemistry?

There was an English teacher who hinted at the "special books" he had locked away in a cupboard. Maybe that was supposed to induce some sort of desire to probe further into literature. One gift he did give me was being forced to learn long passages from Shakespeare's plays and verses from the major poets. I can still remember large chunks of important pieces to this day.

I was lucky because I had discovered a way of remaining fairly anonymous in class so that most of my teachers left me alone. When I was around sixteen, the chemistry teacher suggested there was no point coming to his lessons and I'd be far better off studying on my own. In my final year at school I obtained lecture notes from a friend doing his university degree and worked on that.

"Dickey Blink," the physics teacher, taught me a great deal about critical thinking. In many ways his classes were superior to anything I was to experience at university. Most teachers set up an experiment and then have the students make measurements. Dickey Blink, however, would ask us, for example, to measure the specific heat of copper. He then expected us to work out exactly how we would do the experiment and which pieces of apparatus we would need to take out of the store cupboard. We were then to set this up, as well as working out an estimate of the experimental errors involved. When doing electrical experiments with what is known as a Wheatstone bridge he would creep up behind us and pull out a few wires. We then had to reconnect the circuit without reference to any diagram and, based upon reasoning, work out how the current would flow. Dickey Blink challenged me and made me think. I also discovered how he was able to see out of the back of his head and shout out to a specific boy while apparently focused on writing on the blackboard. In fact he had set up a series of concealed mirrors that allowed him to see what was going on behind him in other parts of the room.

Another major influence was the art master, Mr. Edwards, who became one of the key figures in my education. My aunt, who was an amateur painter of sunsets and picturesque scenes of the Lake District, had sparked my interest in art. She taught me to paint in a similar way, from picture postcards. Later I persuaded her to accompany me on bike rides so we could both sit and paint together before nature.

The art master must have sensed my interest and introduced me to art in a wider sense than Sunday painting. He talked to me about Picasso, Klee and Mondrian. Even more important he didn't speak down to me as if I was a schoolboy but almost as if I were an equal. From time to time he would invite me to look at the work of one of the students he was coaching to enter art school. "Well, Peat, what do you think of that?" he'd ask. We'd stand in silence for some time and in this way I learned how to look. Then would follow one of those curious forms of communication involving gestures, mutual sympathy and very few words.

That passion for looking has remained with me ever since. I have gone to art galleries around the world and in most cases rush through the rooms until I find one painting where I can stand and dialogue for a long time. I ask questions of the painting and slowly it replies. Then it begins to ask questions of me. It may be a still life by Cotán or a Velázquez in Madrid; Seurat's *Bathers* or Piero Della Francesca's *Baptism of Christ* in London's National Gallery, Simone Martini and Duccio in Siena; Jackson Pollock in New York.

Those school days were a period of prolific learning. I needed to escape from the narrowness of my background, the suburbs of Liverpool and the restrictions of my school. Nearly everything I learned took place in those hours when school ended and before I went to sleep. I had to devour the world's literature. I had to read not only the English writers but also the Russians, French, Germans and then Ibsen and Strindberg. I read my way through Dostoevsky late at night, through Fielding and Rabelais–anything I could get my hands on. I was an avid listener of the BBC Third Programme. In its golden age it provided what amounted to a university education with lectures on art, music and science, and plays from Seneca to Harold Pinter. Later it was BBC television's "Monitor" program, in which Ken Russell got his start making marvelous docudramas about Elgar, Bartók, Debussy, Delius and the Pre-Raphaelites.

A good friend of mine, Clem Ford–who is now a professor of linguistics at the university of Montreal–had quit school to work as a grape picker, first in France and then in Spain. He helped fire my passion for French poetry and I improved my French so I could enjoy Baudelaire, Verlaine, Prévert and Villon. I felt I had to get to Paris, which to me seemed home to the avant-garde of artists and writers–but that came a few years later and anyway I was to learn that the heyday of that particular aspect of French culture had long passed. Jack Kerouac's *On the Road* appeared in 1957, a book we devoured in a day and a night when it first came out. Clem and I began to learn of the Beats and San Francisco became our new Mecca. We even made a joke that we'd meet in 1970 in Mexico City–just like Burroughs, Ginsberg and Kerouac had met there in the fifties. This, in fact, was to actually happen. Clem had been working and hitch-hiking around South America. On his way north into Canada to take up a university position, he ran out of money and was forced to stay in Mexico City in a hotel that was being used as a brothel. The year was 1970 and he happened to see a notice for a physics meeting and decided to walk towards the university center. I was attending the conference and walking down the road in the other direction. We met, after not seeing each other for years, as if it was perfectly normal–after all that is how we had planned to meet. We had two great days in Mexico City and I gave him enough money to make it by bus to Canada.

Books have always been important to me and the more I was reading the more I was missing. I spent hours in the local library but began to realize that there were considerable gaps in its collection. Where, for example, were the plays of Tennessee Williams and Arthur Miller? In the end I sent in a letter of complaint to the chief librarian with a list of books I felt should be in the collection. It had slipped my mind that my father was chairman of the library committee. Several evenings later he came home in a black mood. He had been asked to leave the room while they considered a letter written by one of his relations–myself. His greatest shame had occurred when the chief librarian had asked him, "Do you realize your son is requesting books by homosexuals and communists?"

My schooldays were a time to learn about music. With a group of friends we began by collecting 78s of trad jazz. (I wonder how many readers know what a 78 is? A vinyl record that played for around three minutes and rotated at 78 revolutions per minute.) Trad was the British version of New Orleans jazz. That meant Humphrey Littleton, Ken Colyer and Chris Barber. We then moved on, temporarily bypassing the bop revolution, to Dave Brubeck and the MJQ–The Modern Jazz Quartet. The liner notes of one of the MJQ's LPs, one that I still have in my collection, referred to the introduction of "Softly as in a Morning Sunrise" as being an adaptation of one of the canons from Bach's *Musical Offering*. But what was a canon and what did Bach sound like? By good fortune we could borrow records from the public library in Liverpool and so I listened to the *Musical Offering* and began to devour Bach. Bach was my first introduction to classical music. Today, I live not far from a Bach expert, the cellist Hans-Eberhard Dentler, who has solved the enigma of Bach's *Art of Fugue* and is now working on a book about the *Musical Offering*.

From Bach I jumped to Holst's *The Planets*, Stravinsky's *The Rite of Spring*, the Bartók String Quartets, and from Anton von Webern back to Haydn. My pleasure was unsurpassed because I was a total open ear. No one had told me what to listen to, who was good and who was bad. Every new disc was a total surprise and so one day I was to find myself in the same position as those who first heard, and were shocked by, Beethoven's Ninth Symphony.

My friend Clem had been borrowing Symphonies Three, Five and Seven and I would go over to his house, accept a large dose of Scotch from his father and settle down to Beethoven's latest symphony. Then, one day Clem said, "Do you know how many symphonies Beethoven wrote?" I made a guess and Clem replied, "Well, he wrote nine and this is the last one." He put a pile of 78s on his turntable and we sat down to listen together. "Just wait till you get to the last movement," he warned me. And so I listened, and the last movement began and–what's this?...people are singing...this has never happened before...a symphony is supposed to be just an orchestra playing, not singers and a choir! I was totally shocked. I was like the woman at the first performance of a Bach *Passion* who fainted from shock in the church.

Another great enthusiasm was the local tennis club. To the eternal regret of the older members, I became captain of the junior section. The junior membership then grew rapidly and we were allowed the use of the clubroom on Saturdays and Sunday mornings. Rather than focusing on playing tennis we began a poker school, arranged Friday night dances and a series of coach trips. My close friend at that time was Dot Courtie. She and I played tennis, took long walks together and talked about our dreams and aspirations. We were as close as two people could ever be. We spent hours together, standing talking holding our bikes, walking in Sniggery Woods, or at her house while she played the piano. We believed that our tiny group of friends was going to change the world and become some fantastic new movement like the Beats.

After she left school Dot went to Liverpool College of Art. One day she told me she'd met someone really interesting at art school. I felt a bit put out by her enthusiasm for this student who turned out to be John Lennon. A little later she ran off with one of her teachers, Austin Davies, who happened to be the husband of another painter, Beryl Bainbridge, the novelist-to-be. Years later, when I read Bainbridge's *Another Part of the Wood* I realized that the character of Dotty was none other than my old friend Dot.

In this way Dot moved on to Goldsmith's College to study art. I made many visits to London and on one occasion we were all supposed to meet with Lennon but by then he and the Beatles had become too famous. Dot is mentioned in one of the Lennon biographies where her nose is described in an uncomplimentary manner.

The Beatles had cropped up before. Teddy Taylor used to knock around with us for a time before going to Hamburg where he recorded some of the Beatles' songs on an old reel-to-reel machine. I believe he was later able to sell these recordings for a considerable sum. My father also had a young apprentice electrician. One day he informed me, as a cautionary tale, that the apprentice had told him he was going to quit and go with his friends to play in Germany. My father tried to argue him out of such a stupid move and, in the end said, "George Harrison, one day you'll come back to me, crawling on your knees and begging for a job." For my part we had a small "skiffle group" that played at the tennis club. I alternated between mandolin—a curious instrument for a skiffle group but the only one I possessed—and drums, in the sense of things you could hit with drumsticks to make noise. (I was deeply influenced by the film, The *Man with the Golden Arm* with the junkie drummer, Frank Sinatra, being "saved" by Kim Novak.) On another occasion my father told me that Harrison's group were looking for a new drummer but by then I had become interested in jazz and felt myself superior to anything Liverpool could produce.

Then there was the very serious young man who worked in NEMS (North End Music Store) a record store in the center of Liverpool. He rapidly became the butt of our humor. We would go in with very straight faces and ask for absurd but possibly real records, that we insisted we had just heard played on the BBC Third Programme–Bach, played on the euphonium, Alphonse Picou playing the E flat saxophone, Stravinsky actually singing "In Memoriam Dylan Thomas." The butt in question was Brian Epstein, whose father owned the store. We were most surprised when he quit work to manage the Beatles. He appeared so totally "square."

Eventually it was time to leave school and enter Liverpool University. This entailed walking to the bus stop at the end of the street and taking the L2, L4 or L8 bus. My father would munch on his toast and marmalade and ask me, "Which bus will you be taking this morning, David?" "Probably the L4," I might reply. He would nod, "I'll be taking the L2." Possibly my father preferred a little solitude in the morning or maybe he was concerned that I might decide to wear my false beard or a clerical collar to go to university.

There were also political differences to be faced with my father. As a new university student I was not totally happy with my father's decision to embrace the Conservative Party in order to sit on the local council. Around election time he needed my help to knock on doors and distribute flyers. This was accompanied by a strong admonition, "Don't offer any opinion; don't even answer any questions. In fact, don't say anything. Just take their name and address and tell them I will visit them." This would be followed by a long pause, then, "And *don't* take any of your university friends with you."

All in all university was a considerable anticlimax. On being welcomed into the university we were given a pep talk to the effect that we were all researchers together–professors and students all working side by side to discover nature's secrets. But the real division between professors and students was large. Many of the lecturers appeared bored when they gave their courses and spoke as if they'd been saying the same thing year after year after year.

One student claimed to have seen the notes used by one of them that dated back many years and contained the jokes that were to be given at various points in the lecture. Another problem was the size of the classes; they were just too big ever to have a discussion or to ask questions of the lecturer.

One class in particular was swollen by engineering students whose bad reputation, "We are, we are, we are the engineers, we can drink fifty beers," was on a par with that of medical students. At all events this mega session was held in a large hall right under the university clock tower so that the class would erupt with collective rhythmic stamping as the bell began to alert people that the hour was coming up. Then, on the hour, loud shouts of "boing, boing..." Paper airplanes would descend towards the lecturer, maybe even fireworks. To make matters worse the clock was chiming noon!! Pretty soon the lecturer was attended by two bodyguards, heavyset men from the engineering department who patrolled up and down the aisles menacing us with hefty chunks of wood.

The best I could do in the face of all this chaos was to try to set my own course of independent study, seek out friends and form groups of intense talkers and thinkers. While at university we formed a group called SPI (Society For Pseudo-Intellectuals) probably based on something I'd read in Aldous Huxley. Our most noted success was in creating meetings that did not exist. These would be well advertised in advance with posters elaborately created by my friend Stuart Ogilvie. We announced a hunt for otters with dogs, the appearance of a right-wing Tory who would speak on the importance of corporal punishment in schools, a petition to ban G.H. Hardy's *A Course of Pure Mathematics*–the standard textbook of mathematics–on the grounds of obscenity. This was all designed to arouse the anger of more politically correct students who would turn up to such non-existent meetings to protest. Our real meetings, however, were in pubs where we would discuss art, mathematics and everything else under the sun.

My path through university was therefore, as with most other things in my life, unorthodox. I was allowed to skip the first year of lectures but towards the end of my second year I developed a series of panic attacks that made it difficult for me to sit exams. Nevertheless I had technically qualified for an ordinary bachelor's degree, yet lacked a third year of residence. I thus began my course of private study again, reading Dirac's famous book on quantum theory and beginning to worry about the theory's foundations. I had also made contact with one of the theoreticians, Tom Grimley. Grimley had come from Bristol University, which had boasted an impressive theoretical group including Bohm, Fröhlich, Powell and Mott. This impressed me but it had not impressed the great Paul Dirac who once visited Bristol for a conference. Seeking to make conversation with Dirac, Grimley had remarked, "It's hard to believe there are so many great minds in this room." "There aren't," replied Dirac.

During Grimley's introductory lectures to quantum mechanics I began to wonder how one would calculate the energy levels of atoms and worked out a theory on my own applying it to helium and lithium. I took the results to Grimley who said, "Ah, you've discovered the Hartree method. And do you know what these patterns of numbers are?" I shook my head. "They are called matrices."

I also took a course in symbolic logic with a Dr Willy Abraham from Ghana, the man who was reputed to have ghostwritten some of President Nkrumah's works. He became Chancellor of Nkrumah University and as far as I know disappeared after the fall of the government.

I also decided to pursue experimental chemistry and began work that was supposed to lead to a PhD. At first I had hoped that lab work would be a continuation of all the pleasure I had experienced doing experiments in the coal shed at home. One day I was singing to myself as I prepared a solution for measurement. I was cut short by my supervisor who asked me what I was doing. When I replied I was singing because I felt happy, he told me that a laboratory was a serious place of work. No one was to whistle, sing or even laugh in the laboratory. Neither should I be sitting looking into a book. If I had nothing else to do I could polish the bench or clean out a piece of apparatus.

I also learned that the lab prided itself on producing "good experimenters," i.e. those who got nice clean results and were able to make straight-line graphs of their experimental observations with all the points being very close to the line. I could never quite manage to do this and began to get discouraged. The reason was that I had never learned the trick. One PhD student, held up as a paragon, told me that if any of his experiment points didn't quite fall on the ideal line then he'd either omit the result or "compensate" assuming that the chemical solution he had made must be slightly out of date and so his results needed to be corrected until they fitted back on the line. Making things look beautiful on the page was apparently more important that truth. (Of course I have always been rather naïve!)

At all events the results I was getting would certainly not fall on a nice straight line. What I did not suspect at the time was that, in fact, I was dealing with what would now be recognized as a non-linear system. (For the technically minded, I was studying the chemical reaction between solutions of chromium and cobalt that is catalyzed by a solution of silver. The chromium was oxidizing the silver which then oxidized the cobalt.) In such a system, also known as an autocatalytic system, concentrations don't vary in a linear way but can oscillate up and down—hence the fluctuations I was getting in my experimental results, which were rejected as no more than the result of my poor experimental practice. In the end I decided to model the system using a computer. If only I had been part of a more far-seeing group maybe we could have been one of the first to demonstrate non-linear reactions but this was the early sixties. Such ideas had not yet been advanced and would certainly have appeared too radical to "good experimentalists."

That brings me to another point; in most cases scientists see what they expect to see. Or rather they have theories and methods that allow them to make calculations for certain types of systems. These theories then become ways of seeing. To take one example, for centuries scientists were able to make calculations for nice simple, linear systems that were always close to equilibrium. This meant that everything they saw around them was linear and near to equilibrium. Anything else, anything that didn't fit into that way of seeing and calculating, was dismissed as an anomaly. But then chaos theory came along, a way of dealing with non-linear systems and systems that are far from equilibrium. Suddenly scientists began to see chaos, complexity and fractals everywhere—from the stock market to clouds, mountains and insect populations.

Now I began to work on a computer called DEUCE that had just been installed at the University. DEUCE was the offspring of ACE (Automatic Computing Engine) built at London's National Physical Laboratory under Alan Turing. It was constructed using electrical valves (or vacuum tubes) with a large rotating drum for its memory. It was the sort of computer you could walk inside and stand up in. Its short-term memory consisted of a series of tubes containing mercury, called delay lines, which were located around the room like mushrooms. Sets of binary numbers were converted into sound waves that moved through the liquid mercury at speeds much slower than in the electronic circuitry, hence creating a short term memory.

I wanted this computer to solve a series of coupled differential equations and so every instruction had to be punched into a hole in a card—such cards also came to be used as household bills marked "Do not bend, fold or mutilate." Then one sat back and watched it calculate. But if the calculation went on too long then the computer would start to overheat and the result would go haywire.

Maybe I should say one more thing about the computer before I leave it behind. To get to the university from my home in Waterloo I sometimes took the bus with a man known as "Old Mister Babbage." He was a nice old man who told me stories of an ancestor of his who was an inventor and fascinated by all sorts of things. Old Mr. Babbage told me that he had some papers in his house with drawings of inventions and one of them was for making calculations. Only later, after he had died, I began to ask around and discovered that he had been a direct descendent of Charles Babbage, the Victorian father of the modern computer.

My work with the computer was motivated by a desire to complete my experimental work and put it behind me. A few months earlier our group faced a small theoretical problem involving the way molecular spectra of solutions change with temperature. Rather than take it to a theoretician I said I'd try to solve it myself. This became my first published work. I showed the answer to Grimley who suggested I abandon the experimental PhD and quickly write up my experimental research for a Master's degree. Then I would come to work with him as a theoretician for my PhD.

Now out of the laboratory I had the task of catching up on all the mathematics I would have needed if I'd originally taken a more orthodox path. I had the pleasure of attending lectures and seminars by Herbert Fröhlich (the physicist who first applied quantum field theory to solid state physics and a pioneer in the theory of superconductivity). I also took the train to Manchester to attend seminars in the theoretical physics department of the university. A new education had begun.

QUANTUM STRANGENESS

Excursion II

S cientists, through the concepts they develop and the technology that flows from such concepts, have an enormous influence in the world. It is therefore ironic that their education should give no attention to the social and ethical implications of the very science they practice. For example, while at university it is extremely rare to be told anything about the history of the subject. I cannot speak for biology but physics and chemistry are generally taught in the abstract. Laws and theories are imparted but without any sense of how those laws came about and through which intellectual tradition they evolved.

Take quantum theory. A student is taught the basic axioms of the theory and then shown how to make calculations of, for example, the spectrum of the hydrogen atom, the conductivity of electricity in a metal, the structure of a chemical bond or what happens when two elementary particles collide at high speed. But nowhere is one taught what the theory actually "means."

When I heard my first lectures on quantum theory at university I was not at all satisfied to be given a set of axioms to learn—that is, those axioms on which the theory is built. I was not really that interested in learning how to calculate the spectrum of hydrogen. Instead I wanted to know what the theory really meant. And so I turned to Dirac's book on quantum theory and puzzled over its first pages. I wanted to know the how and why of the theory. I really wanted to understand it. I needed to ask questions about the way probability was being used, for example. But when I asked my fellow students as well as some who were finishing their PhDs, the answer I received was, "Don't bother. You're wasting your time. No one asks questions like that. You're supposed to use the theory to make calculations."

Understanding the theory and its deeper meaning is far more interesting than simply using it to solve problems about the nature of solids, nuclei, molecules and elementary particles. It is interesting because quantum theory has totally revolutionized the way we think about the world. Take something as simple as an observation of some quantum system. If you think about it a little then you realize that you, or your experimental apparatus, could be said to have made a measurement only if something changes. A meter may move, a Geiger counter may click, something gets written on the hard disc of a computer or a memory is laid down in your brain. For any of these changes to occur there must have been some flow of energy. Energy transforms the states of matter and if no energy flows or is exchanged then a meter, a thermometer, the hard disc of a computer, will all remain unchanged.

When you make a scientific observation in the large scale, such as measuring the temperature of a cup of coffee, these energy exchanges are so miniscule as to be neglected. (The mercury moves in the thermometer because some heat has been taken from the coffee to warm up the thermometer, which then causes the mercury to expand. But the amount of energy exchanged is negligible when compared to the energy in the cup of hot coffee.) Not so at the quantum scale of things. Even the most refined possible measurement will involve the exchange of at least one quantum of energy. But a quantum cannot be divided; it cannot be shared or split in two. This means that at the moment of measurement this quantum is being shared by both the apparatus and quantum system. This implies that the entire system becomes an undivided whole—because a quantum is indivisible you cannot analyze or split apart the system and observer in any way. Only after the measurement has ended, and the large-scale apparatus has changed, can you speak of two separate systems. The essence of quantum theory at the moment of observation is that of "undivided wholeness."

This is something radically new in science. The physicist John Wheeler put it this way, "We had this old idea that there was a universe out there and me, the observer, safely protected by a six-inch slab of plate glass. Now we have to shatter the plate glass; we have to reach in there…the old word *observer* has to be crossed off the books and we must put in the new word *participator*."

Of course the effect of the observer is also true in our large-scale world. If you watch children playing you make them self-conscious and change their behavior. If you want to cheat at golf you praise your opponent's drive and ask him exactly how he makes the swing—a ruse guaranteed to put him off his stroke.

But there is more to learn of the quantum world. Take Heisenberg's uncertainty principle, for example. One sort of measurement will tell us about the speed of an electron. Another sort of measurement will tell us where it is—its position. Yet quantum nature places a limit as to the precision with which we can know both position and speed. That is, there is a fundamental uncertainty, and no matter what we do, no matter how refined a measurement is made this uncertainty cannot be reduced below a certain level.

When Heisenberg uncovered this relationship within the equations of quantum theory he interpreted it in the following way. Suppose I have determined the position of an electron. Now I observe its speed and in so doing I disturb the electron's position a little and make it uncertain. But suppose I go back to measure that position again? In doing so I now disturb its speed. For Heisenberg each observation of a quantum system acts to disturb its inherent properties.

On the surface this sounds reasonable but it is to ignore the inherent wholeness in quantum theory. In fact the physicist Niels Bohr summoned Heisenberg to Copenhagen and remonstrated with him to the point where he had the younger man in tears. Bohr pointed out that Heisenberg had begun with the assumption that there, in fact, exist well-defined objects, i.e. electrons that "possess" intrinsic properties. When we measure one of these properties, Heisenberg assumed, we disturb the other intrinsic property. In other words, the electron itself had well-defined properties when we are not observing it. But there is a limit to which we, in our large-scale world, can come to know these intrinsic properties.

Bohr turned this on its head. The electron does not "possess" properties, he argued. It is our act of observation, the apparatus we use, that sets up the conditions under which nature gives us an answer which we call "speed." Another arrangement will yield a number we interpret as "position." But these do not exist outside the experiment. They are a product of the interaction between the observer and the observed.

We are no longer the impartial observers of an objective universe. Ours is now a participatory universe. When we interrogate the universe the questions we ask help to form the answers we are given. Quantum nature is holistic. It is not a machine composed out of the interaction of independent parts. Rather it is closer to a process, to something inherently organic, than to a Newtonian clockwork.

Yet another area in which quantum theory surprises us is at the level of chance. A substance is radioactive because the center of each atom, its nucleus, contains, for example, too many neutrons. (The components of a nucleus are electronically charged protons and electrically neutral neutrons held together by the attractive forces of mesons.) It can achieve stability by shooting away one of these surplus neutrons. Very unstable radioactive substances decay quickly; others take years or centuries to decay.

Where chance comes in, is in the fact that you can never predict when one particular nucleus will decay. If you have a box containing a million atoms you can predict that at the end of one hour, say, half a million will have decayed leaving a half-million unstable ones around. At the end of another hour there will be a quarter of a million unstable nuclei–and so on. But if you look at an individual nucleus you don't know if it will decay in the next minute, next hour or next day! The moment it decays is governed by pure chance. This is something hard to accept for physics has always dealt in causal and reproducible laws. Radioactivity is profoundly different. Each is a singular, unpredictable event.

Finally there is Bohr's principle of complementarity. The French physicist Louis de Broglie had proposed that the electron has both a wave-like and a particle-like nature. This was later confirmed by experiment–just as it was shown that light has both a wave-like and a particle-like nature. But a wave is an extended thing and a particle is a localized thing. The two descriptions appear incompatible.

This is where Bohr's complementarity comes in. He suggested that the quantum world is so rich that no single description can exhaust a phenomenon; rather there must be complementarity and even paradoxical descriptions. Bohr also felt that this notion of complementarity applies equally well to the mind. Wolfgang Pauli, for example, pointed out that a particular content of the mind can have a conscious quality that we are aware of and an unconscious or symbolic quality that only appears in dreams. Each is one aspect of a certain level of reality but both cannot be experienced at one and the same time.

So quantum theory presents us with a radically new vision of the world. We must now accept a level of chance and uncertainty. Physics cannot offer a more complete description. We must not only accept a limit to what we can know with total precision about the quantum world, but also what we can say about the very nature of quantum reality. Finally we have come to learn that we live in a participatory universe. These are deep changes and the physicists Wolfgang Pauli and Niels Bohr suggested that there are profound connections between the way the mind works and the quantum level.

RESEARCH AND DIVERSIONS

Chapter 3

I was happy to be doing theoretical research and spent the first few months looking at various problems and picking up techniques. It had been the tradition of Fröhlich–and my thesis supervisor Grimley was of the same school–that students should discover their own problem and find out what was of particular interest to them.

And so I studied, talked to people, went to seminars and begin to tease out what I should be doing. Since it is rather technical in nature maybe it should be left to the next Excursion, the one that follows this chapter.

So let me return to university in general. It is a unique time in life; you are no longer a child going to school and answerable to parents, nor a full adult with all the responsibilities of a job, mortgage and the rest. For me it was an interlude: one in which I could explore things and generally wander around. The French have a great verb for this activity, or non-activity, *flâner*. One of the things I would do was take the ferry across the River Mersey–later made famous in song by Gerry and the Pacemakers. Partly it was to revive fond memories of ferry trips with my uncle who still had a yearning for the sea. He would hang around the entrance to the engine room and then say, "Wait here a moment, David, I'm just going down to talk." And down he would go to reminisce about engines and innovations. I especially liked taking the ferry in winter to New Brighton, because at that time of the year the amusement park was closed. I loved to wander through the deserted fairground, the colored lights extinguished, the rides covered, the stalls boarded over, but a special magic remaining in the air.

In the summer I would go to my father's cottage in North Wales with an old school friend, Bill Mulligan. Bill and I went fly fishing in the tiny River Leet at the bottom of the road, "Ah, flogging the river are you, boys?" Then in the evening we would light the gas lamps and sit by the fire to talk late, late into the night. Such talks we had.

I was also enjoying the concerts at the Liverpool Philharmonic Hall because we were lucky to have John Pritchard as a conductor who began to introduce contemporary music into his program. Liverpool was also a center for theaters including a resident company at the Liverpool Playhouse, a place were a number of well-known actors had made their start. There was something particular about Liverpool and language. Maybe it was the mixture of English, Welsh and Irish as well as all those other races that enter and leave a major port. The particular Liverpudlian dialect called "scouse" was ideally geared for humor and the deflating of the pompous. I remember the reply of a black bus conductor with a strong scouse accent who had been insulted by a passenger, "My father used to eat people like you," he said. Scouse humor was present in the Beatles and several leading British comedians have been born and bred in Liverpool. It was also home to the "Liverpool Poets," Adrian Henri, Roger McGough and Brian Patten who gave "Poetry and Jazz" readings.

And then we had a new American influence, Sam Wanamaker, who opened a theater in Liverpool called the Everyman. Sam brought in top actors from the United States for the modern American classics–Tennessee William's *Rose Tattoo* with Anna Magnani, and Arthur Miller's *View from the Bridge* and *Death of a Salesman*. What's more he opened lunchtime poetry readings where people could sit with their sandwiches. Later Wanamaker moved to London and was the driving force in having Shakespeare's Globe Theatre rebuilt.

This was also the time I began to write. I had written sprawling adventure stories at primary school and later, going into the local library, I had this fantasy of writing the sorts of science books that I wanted to read. Now I began to write in a series of notebooks. I have them here in my office now, a vast collection tottering on top of the bookcase and about to crash down at any moment. I wrote down what I had been thinking over the past days. I wrote down ideas. I wrote short pieces of fiction, reportage, and poetry. I was experimenting in how to put things down on paper. At one point I read a magazine article by Kerouac, about the way he wrote; a sort of stream of consciousness typed directly onto the page. I tried that. Later I was to learn that you could only do that effectively once you've mastered the art of using words. Let me give you an example. A poet friend of mine went to the Jack Kerouac School of Disembodied Poetics at Boulder, Colorado, to take a course with the Beat poet Allen Ginsberg. To his surprise he was asked to write a poem that adhered strictly to the sonnet form. Ginsberg insisted that he do this over and over again. Only when he had mastered form, Ginsberg said, had he earned the right to experiment.

Then there was astronomy or at least the fiction of astronomy. The astronomical society at Liverpool University was filled with serious students whose great passion was to look at double stars. As far as I was concerned if I saw one double star then I'd seen them all. So why did my friend and I join? Because one privilege of membership was to obtain the key to an observatory located in the next town along the coast, Southport. The facility had been closed as a working observatory but could still be used by members of the astronomical society. What's more it was in the center of a secluded park. In other words, an ideal location in which to organize parties. And so we astronomers would go to the local off-license to stock up on fortified wines, "None of your lunatic's broth here, boys," the licensee would assure us. Armed with a few bottles and a portable record player we set ourselves up in the observatory. There we held a number of parties and on one occasion received a visit from the police who came banging on the door at the base of the observatory. My friend, Ogilvie confronted them. He was very good at assuming a pompous and authoritative air, even after several glasses of British sherry-type wine.

"What's all the noise? What are you doing in there?" asked the police constable.

"We are astronomers," Ogilvie answered.

'But what are you doing?"

"We are observing the tides on the moon." The officer went away bewildered but satisfied.

There was also art—which had long been my passion. A man named John Moores had made his fortune running football pools, and now funded an annual exhibition of contemporary art at Liverpool's Walker Art Gallery. There I came into contact with the work of leading contemporary British artists and at the same time met a couple of artists who became friends. With one of these we began to explore the whole area of art and science, which interests me to this day. How do artists see the world and is it the same as the scientist's vision? Does beauty in art have anything to do with beauty or elegance in science and mathematics? Roger Penrose, the mathematician, once told me that when mathematicians don't know what to do next they should try to do the most beautiful thing possible. In this way beauty becomes a means to an end and an end in itself. But is this sense of beauty identical to that experienced by an artist?

The marriage of art and science remains a great dream for me and some of my most satisfying discussions have been with artists whom I respect. On the other hand I am forced to say that "art and science" did become a fashion for a time and quite a lot of money was pumped in that direction. Yet in so many cases the results were disappointing, there seemed to be no true and deep engagement. An artist wasn't being taken beyond his or her current position by discussions with scientists. Scientists, for their part, seemed untouched by the experiments of artists. What was produced in so many cases was nothing more than a series of uninteresting illustrations of scientific ideas, or the exploitation of new materials and technologies simply because they happened to be around. Later on in this book I'll give an example of how the injection of a very small amount of money in a sensitive way produced something very interesting.

All this leads me to a question I asked while at a conference where so many neuroscientists, psychologists, etc. were carrying out research in fields related to love and altruism. "Why are so many of you doing this?" I asked. "Because that's where the money is," came the reply. Exactly the same answer given by Bonnie and Clyde when they were asked why they robbed banks. The true marriage of art and science can never be catalyzed by money. While funding is important, it must always be a by-product of something much deeper. True engagement only comes about when an artist is deeply involved in a personal dialogue with science, or when a scientist needs to move beyond a present fixed position in order to embrace something essential about art.

And now on to France. At that time during my research I must have been a little like one of those characters in Julian Barnes' novel, *Metroland*. Anything to do with France was exotic. My spoken French was not that great but I could read Camus, Cocteau's plays and the poetry of Villon, Baudelaire, Verlaine, Rimbaud, Aragon. And France had been home to the Impressionists and the Surrealists. I'd also heard about Jean-Paul Sartre and the Existentialists. I wasn't quite sure of their philosophy at the time except that it appeared to involve a great deal of talking, Juliette Gréco, dressing in dark clothes, listening to modern jazz, snapping one's fingers to applaud and drinking coffee in late night bars…the list went on, so Paris was obviously the place to go.

On my first trip to Paris I stayed in a hotel on the Rue Blanche in Montmartre. I would wander around the district at night, climbing to Sacré-Coeur to see the lights of Paris below. I visited all the jazz clubs in Paris. At that time union restrictions in England limited the amount of American jazz we could hear. This did not apply in Paris. I went to the Blue Note and sat a few feet away from Bud Powell. (Later I was to enjoy the film *Round Midnight*, in which the character based on the real-life Powell had been transformed from pianist to saxophonist.) The night I attended the club it was fairly empty. Most people were talking and so I took a table on the stage itself where I could focus on Powell who actually nodded and smiled at me–probably I was the only one in the club paying serious attention. Paris was everything I had hoped it would be.

THE MANY-BODY PROBLEM

Excursion III

I've now come to an excursion that is more technical and difficult to follow than some of the others. So you, dear reader, are perfectly free to skip ahead to the next chapter if you wish. The theoretical research program I was engaged in under Grimley fell under the generic title of "the many-body problem." It is one of the outstanding problems of theoretical physics and goes back to the time of Isaac Newton. In 1684, the astronomer Edmond Halley (best known for the discovery of Halley's comet) visited Newton and posed to him the problem of how a planet orbits the sun. Newton told him he had already solved the problem and would send him the results. Later this was to form an important part of Newton's *Principia*. With his three laws of motion and his theory of universal gravitation he was able to prove that bodies that experience an inverse square law of attraction make closed elliptical orbits.

Newton could prove this for two bodies–earth and sun, for example–but not for three. For example he couldn't solve the sun-earth-moon system nor the sun-Jupiter-asteroid belt system. Instead astronomers were forced to make use of a series of successive approximations, called perturbation theory. The assumption was that perturbations are a series of small corrections to the known two-body solution. The pull of the moon as it goes round the earth doesn't have too great an effect on the earth's orbit around the sun. Yes, there certainly would be a small effect but astronomers were confident that they could calculate the correction, and even the correction to that correction, without too much difficulty. The same applied to other planets and moons in the solar system. In each case the extra body would produce small changes in a planetary orbit. But not everyone was happy with this approach. After all one is adding up corrections to corrections to corrections and, in principal at least, there could be an infinite number of such corrections. This was what bothered the mathematician Henri Poincaré. In 1900 he managed to demonstrate that in most cases the cumulative effect of these corrections is generally small–as expected. However under certain critical situations the sets of corrections begin to blow up to the point that a planet may fly out of the solar system altogether or even behave in a chaotic manner.

But 1900 was also the year of Max Planck's hypothesis of the quantum and five years later, in 1905, Einstein came up with the theory of relativity. It is probably for these reasons, and the immense mathematical difficulties involved in going any further, that Poincaré's result remained relatively ignored until the sudden explosion of interest that took place in the second half of the twentieth century. The name of this new interest was chaos theory.

What applied to the earth and sun also applied to a lone electron rotating around a proton–in short to the hydrogen atom. Quantum theory could be used to calculate exactly the energy levels of hydrogen. But what of helium with two electrons, or lithium with three? What about the hydrogen molecule–two nuclei linked together by a pair of electrons? And what of the astronomical number of electrons in a metal?

This was the many-body problem of quantum theory. How were physicists to calculate the spectrum of larger atoms and compare them with accurate experiments? How could chemists study the bonding between various elements to produce molecules? How could physicists understand the transport of heat and electricity within a metal? How could chemists understand the catalytic effect of a platinum surface on certain reactions?

At that time scientists were forced to use perturbation theory in the context of quantum theory, making an initial calculation then adding in a series of corrections. This could be programmed into a computer whose power and memory would today be dwarfed by the cheapest PC clone.

All this seemed like no more than brute force to me. Certainly you came up with a numerical solution. But what was the point? There seemed to be nothing creative in it, nothing new, no deep physical principles. One simply "turned the handle" as it were. Where was the fun in that? Where was the challenge?

As it turned out I was pretty naïve in believing that scientific research should be fun. I should have been warned by the occasion when I was caught singing while doing an experiment. On another occasion an older theoretical physicist gave me fatherly advice. "Find some small problem, discover a technique for solving it, and continue to publish for five or ten years until you have established a reputation. Only then can you afford to think about the things that really interest you." When I looked around I did see that many people were working on "little problems." Their research would gain them tenure and promotion because of the number of papers they could publish.

Now I'd better talk about density matrices and, since most people will not be at all interested in density matrices, I'll remind them again that they'd be well-advised to skip the next few paragraphs and start reading again where something more interesting comes along!

When physicists deal with an atom or molecule they work with that they call its wave function. The wave function is the most complete description of a pure quantum state. Yet the wave function contains too much information. We know about atoms and molecules because of the observations we make. Every observation produces a result, a set of numbers. These sets of numbers can be calculated using the wave function. But it turns out that these same numbers can also be calculated exactly using a vastly simpler function called the reduced density matrix.

For an atom containing n electrons you require a wave function containing $3n$ coordinates. But for the reduced density matrix, or 2-matrix, you only need four coordinates. The density matrix contains a lot less information than a wave function. In computer terms it is a sort of "zipped" or "compressed" wave function. Yet it contains all the information we need to know about the results of any observation. All the physics you will ever need about a system is contained in this compressed form, the reduced density matrix.

I found that very interesting, the notion that the physics of a situation is enfolded within the density matrix. It also has great practical implications because it means one can store exact information about a quantum system in a compressed form. This means that incredibly difficult computer calculations could now be performed with ease. There was only one fly in the ointment. It is called the N-Representability problem.

As we have seen, a reduced density matrix is a highly compressed version of the wave function. But which wave function? How can we be sure that it has been compressed from exactly the right wave function? This is the N-Representability problem: how to discover all the conditions that must be placed on a trial density matrix to ensure it has been zipped down from a well-behaved wave function. It's not at all difficult to come up with all manner of *necessary* conditions, i.e. properties that the reduced density matrix should have, but to find one that is *sufficient,* i.e. definitive, is a different matter. A density matrix that satisfied a number of *sufficient* conditions may or may not be zipped down from a wave function with the correct symmetry but one that satisfies *necessary* conditions certainly will. Scientists had no problem coming up with sufficient conditions; the necessary ones eluded them.

I thought it was not so much a problem as a clue. It was telling us of the deep significance of symmetry in quantum theory. Wave functions for electrons must be what are known as antisymmetric. The N-Representability problem asks how we know if a trial density matrix has really been compressed from a wave function of that symmetry. Antisymmetry also means that a wave function cannot be separated into independent parts. This has a very important physical consequence. It tells us that two electrons can never be totally independent no matter how far apart they are separated. In fact they must always be correlated. This is known as Bell's theorem. It has now been demonstrated experimentally and tells us that quantum theory is non-local; it transcends the normal restrictions of space and time. Clearly there is a deep connection between N-Representability and Bell's theorem. This early piece of research taught me that by going deeper and deeper into any problem one realizes how significant the connections are to many other areas of physics.

OH CANADA!

Chapter 4

Time had passed and I was now writing up my PhD thesis. The next step was to take a two-year postdoctoral. But where? Paris meant a great deal to me and I knew that Louis de Broglie was at the Henri Poincaré Institute, a place where people thought seriously about the philosophical issues of quantum theory. One evening, while listening to the BBC Third Programme, I'd heard someone called David Bohm being interviewed. He excited my interest because he was talking in a very different way from anyone else I'd heard. He was going deeply into new ideas about physics and I learned that he had contact with the Poincaré Institute and was working on a new theory with de Broglie's assistant Jean Vigier. Then there was also the possibility of continuing my density matrix work with Roy McWeeny in England. I toyed with that idea but decided that I wanted to leave England for a little in order to see something more of the world

I looked into the University of California at San Diego. It didn't look too far, on my map at least, from San Francisco which, as everyone knew, was "home of the Beats." The people at San Diego were also doing some interesting work and the climate would be a great change after cold and rainy Liverpool.

Then I saw an advertisement for fellowships at Queen's University in Canada. One of the topics mentioned was "density matrices," exactly my field. Canada wasn't Paris. Neither was it San

Francisco. On the other hand I'd been impressed by the ending of the movie *Scott of the Antarctic*, with men fighting the bitter cold and sleeping in tents. I assumed that Canada must be like that. This ignorant prejudice was confirmed by the sorts of photographs displayed on the walls of the Canadian Consulate in Liverpool and the information sheet they provided with stories of bear and moose walking down the main streets of Canadian cities.

But there was something else. Some years earlier I had seen a television documentary on the Canadian pianist, Glenn Gould. Gould was a truly exceptional musician. To hear even the first notes of the "Goldberg" Variations or the *Well-tempered Clavier* is to know for certain that Gould is playing and bringing a unique interpretation. Gould was also a considerable eccentric, sitting on a low rickety wooden chair to play, moaning and groaning, sometimes conducting himself. He was a recluse who spent the night on the telephone to his friends. There are legends about his public performances. How, during a piano concerto, the conductor was so struck by the interpretation that he left the podium and sat in the audience to listen.

Then Gould abruptly abandoned the stage for the studio. Public performance for Gould had always held an element of dishonesty. He preferred the seclusion of the studio where he could work on alternative takes and begin to splice his performance together. He even imagined the future of music in which the listener would be supplied with data containing alternative tempos, orchestral accompaniment, and solo interpretations. In this way the listener would no longer be passive but could create his or her unique interpretation.

And so I watched the documentary and learned about Gould. I saw him at his piano in his lakeside cottage north of Toronto. Gould and the Canadian countryside seemed to merge together and become expressions of each other. There was a vision, a dream here, an expression of genius and the spirit of place. Another reason to be in Canada.

And what of scientific research? John Coleman was at Queen's and he had done some of the most interesting work on what is known as the N-Representability problem for density matrices. And so it was to be two years at Queen's University in Canada.

But before leaving I wanted to meet the philosopher Bertrand Russell. I drove to the small Welsh seaside town of Port Merion, which was to become famous as the setting for an innovative television series "The Prisoner." I looked up his name in the phone book and during the subsequent telephone conversation Russell invited me to afternoon tea in his house above the bay. He had no idea who I was but appeared quite happy to chat. He told me it was increasingly difficult for him to sleep. He did no more philosophy but read detective stories late into the night. At that time he was deeply concerned about the arms race and was writing to many of the world's leaders. As to nationalism, he had no time for that and told me the story of the woman he had met while attending the UN in Geneva, who was a representative of a small emerging nation. One day, while cycling down a steep hill towards a traffic intersection, she discovered that the brakes on her bicycle would not work. "What did you do? How did you feel?" asked Russell. "I thought of my country," was the reply that, to Russell, was the epitome of the stupidity that assails the world.

Russell's mind was still agile, although his deafness made conversation difficult at times. He must have been asked the same questions over and over again so tended to assume the question and occasionally trot out well-worn answers. When he learned that I was going to Canada he asked me to do all that was possible for peace. Then Lady Russell came in and served China tea. Before I left he stood up and looked through his picture windows out over the bay. This seemed an important gesture–a man high above the world, close to death, looking out over the sea.

After that I was free to leave England, for a time at least as I fully expected to be back after two years. I took a flight to Montreal and spent the night in a cheap hotel room. The next day I caught the train to Kingston, staring out of the window in the hope of seeing herds of moose, roaming bear, caribou, and the like. Arriving in Kingston I took a cab to the university which I discovered was closed because of a public holiday. A janitor directed me to a "greasy spoon" nearby and after drinking a coffee I saw above the counter a notice, "Rest Rooms Upstairs." How civilized Canada was proving to be, to provide little rooms with beds where one could doze for an hour or two in the afternoon. That, along with flannels, torches, boots of cars, petrol and being "knocked up" in the morning, was to show me that Canadian English was not quite the same as that spoken in England. (Later I was also to learn that while the American accent varies from place to place it also differs from the Canadian in the pronunciation of the diphthong *ou* as in *house* and *about*. One of my daughters once did voice-overs in Canada for an American cartoon series and after the tapes had been delivered to Los Angeles, she was instructed to go back into the studio and redo, with an American accent, every sentence that contained such words!)

Queen's University and Kingston became my new home. It was also the place where my first two children, Sarah and Jason, were born. In Kingston I was free to follow my research wherever it led. I could also attend the density matrix seminars held by John Coleman and talk to his students and colleagues. Pretty soon Coleman was organizing a summer school where I was to meet most of the leading figures in the field.

As to Queen's itself? It was a university with a very active life. What's more, Kingston was also home to Canada's Royal Military College and to a school of nursing, so that the small town was packed with students. In the summer, students congregated along the shore of Lake Ontario to lie in the sun, read and talk. Sometime I even gave my seminars by the lakeside. At night one could walk down any street and come upon a party, the door open in welcome and the sounds of the Beatles, Mamas and Papas or the Doors reaching out into the road.

In many ways I felt I had come to paradise. I'd also found artists to hang out with; that link between art and science was always important to me. I tried writing poetry and short pieces of fiction. I carried physics books home with me to study in the evening. All in all I was having a pretty good time.

Kingston was also the spot that introduced me to the sun. I had read of Van Gogh, brought up in Holland and first discovering the power of the sun at Arles. The sun entered his paintings and changed everything for him. Likewise I had been brought up in Liverpool where it was either overcast or raining. (In "Strawberry Fields," the Beatles have a line about getting a tan from standing in the English rain.) Anyway Kingston introduced me to the power of the sun for the first time in my life. And how easy it was to recognize an arrival from England on the beach. Their blue-white skin would soon turn bright red and then peel! Now it would be hard for me to live away from the sun. In our present house in Pari, Italy I can sit on the balcony and face south with the sun on my face in January and February

My intention had been to return to England and maybe join the density matrix group headed by Roy McWeeny–who now, by a remarkable coincidence, lives in Pisa, not too far from Pari, and is a strong supporter of our Center here. So in that sense the contact worked out fine–but thirty years later. As it turned out, at the end of two years, instead of going back to England I found myself in Ottawa at the National Research Council of Canada. At that time, the late 1960s, it had an excellent reputation, and a Nobel Prize had been given to Gerhard Herzberg in the physics division for his work on spectroscopy. It seemed like an ideal place to continue research.

But the town of Ottawa, at least as it was during that period, bored me. In Kingston I had been part of a lively student community. Now I was in the heart of a civil service town. A major interest became the friends I made at the National Gallery of Canada and the various artists they brought in–Dan Flavin, Michael Snow, Jim Rosenquist and others from Canada and the US.

On the other hand there was the land itself. A short drive north from Ottawa brought me to the lakes and hills of the Gatineau Park. Then there were those weeks and weekends camping out by a lake or river. Winter was cold, very cold but for a time I had a dog who would encourage me to go on walks in the snow. I also bought a pair of cross-country skis. That is really the only way to survive a Canadian winter–engage in outdoor sports and activities. I even tried skating but was told I looked too much like an Englishman.

But there was another side to winter–the driveway. At some point towards the end of November there would be the first snowfall of the year. Generally several feet. And this meant that the driveway had to be cleared in order to park the car. Of course those who worked in offices often had been inactive over the summer and so there were the usual newspaper stories of people who had suffered a heart attack while digging the snow. That was my nagging vision of the future–lying on my back in a snowdrift. Snow falling into my face. The world slowly fading out into blackness.

I continued with my research and a series of postdoctoral students passed through my office. In addition, I took on a graduate student, David Schrum, whom I had met at Queen's. On one occasion, while I was working on density matrices there, he had written quite a complicated computer program for me, which we ran over many hours. Now he wanted to work on a PhD. We discussed a variety of problems and one of the things we talked about was what happens at the surface of a metal. Metals have a regular lattice structure with the centers of atoms located in very regular patterns and electrons moving relatively freely within this metal lattice. (When you switch on the light a current of electrons flows through the metal wire, bumping into the atoms and causing them to vibrate. The end result is that the vibrating metal lattice heats up and energy is given off in the form of light–the bulb glows white.)

But what happens when electrons reach the edge, i.e. the surface of a metal? It's at this point that interesting things happen and the surface of a metal can be quite active and even act as a catalyst for chemical reactions. At all events many people had worked on this problem of what are known as "surface states." But now Schrum came up with an interesting idea–what about the plasma in a metal? A plasma is a gas of charged particles. Plasmas are found at the surface of stars and in outer space. It is also the case that the gas of electrons in a metal acts like a plasma, a theory first proposed by David Bohm. Schrum intended to go back to Bohm's original work–which assumed a metal of infinite dimensions–but this time add the effect of a surface. This seemed a very interesting approach and we had many exciting discussions.

As to my own research I had moved on from density matrices to problems in solid-state physics. But the more I carried on, and the more I talked to the postdoctoral fellows, the more I realized I was not fully engaged. Each day I was becoming more and more frustrated. Theoretically we were supposed to sign in and out of the building, but on some days I would climb out of the window of my ground floor office and wander around by the Rideau River and waterfall, or take a book to read in the sun. I decided to go back to the fathers of twentieth century science and read the seminal papers of Dirac, Bohr, Heisenberg, Pauli, Fermi and Einstein–and even earlier to Maxwell and Newton's *Principia*.

Unlike those who study literature, anyone seriously working in science probably never goes back to read those original works. Every physicist fully understands Newton's three laws of motion but may never know what Newton actually wrote about them and the assumptions he made along the way. Now I was going back in time and coming into contact with the finest minds of science. I saw the way they faced a problem fully and clearly. I realized what it meant when someone had to go to the heart of nature for the very first time. Everything that came afterwards–for those who followed the great innovators–was refinement, dotting i's and crossing t's, finding a "little problem" and working on it for five or ten years.

Doing science, I felt, should be fun. It wasn't just another job, it had to be engaging. It should challenge one's creativity. Science is about celebrating the universe. It's about seeing beyond the appearance of things to what lies within. It is understanding the symmetries and patterns of the world. It is the delight in discovering the unexpected, the particular, and the individual. The English poet, Gerard Manley Hopkins, came close to expressing what I was feeling at the time when he spoke of "inscape"–that inner authenticity of individual things. In this I am reminded of the Sufi story of the master who was ready to pass on his mantle to one of his students. He had decided on a rather unprepossessing boy, a choice his wife thought would be a stupid mistake. And so the master announced that on the following day each student should bring him a gift. The next day they arrived bearing flowers, bowls of perfect fruit and so on. But his favorite student came empty handed.

"Why have you brought me nothing?" the master asked.

"I went out into the fields and saw some wild flowers," the young man said, "but just as I bent to pick them they sang the praises of Allah and so I passed them by. Then I went to pick fruit from a tree but that too sang the praises of Allah. Wherever I went everything sang the praises of Allah and so I have returned empty handed."

I have always felt a sense of wonder at being a corporal being in the natural world. As a child I enjoyed the feel of dirt under my fingers when I played in the garden. At one and the same time I wanted to celebrate the physical presence of the world, but also to understand what lay below, to understand what had been hidden. Every question one probes reveals another level, a deeper question, and beyond that yet another and another. This was the road I was taking into physics.

I had to go to the essential issues of quantum theory and relativity. I needed to understand why these great theories had never been unified. Each one was incredibly successful and in a certain sense each depended upon the existence of the other yet despite the best efforts of scientists over the decades the two refused to marry. But now I had a sabbatical year coming up and I could do something about it. I wrote around for advice asking who was doing the most interesting work in the fields of quantum theory and relativity. The answer came back: Roger Penrose. At that time he was head of the mathematics department at Birkbeck College, University of London.

Penrose and Stephen Hawking had been working together on the theory of black holes and, after hearing a talk by John Wheeler, I became interested in thermodynamic considerations of black holes and ways in which it may be possible for energy to escape. I wrote a short paper for *Nature* suggesting that energy could indeed radiate from a black hole. Penrose himself also had one foot in relativity and the other in quantum theory. He seemed like an ideal choice and so I decided to go to London for the start of my sabbatical.

Accommodation was not easy to find but in the end my family moved into a tiny porter's flat in one of the residences of Goldsmith's College in south London. The building itself was otherwise occupied by female students, many of whom were specializing in music or art. This meant that I could sit in a rehearsal room and listen to a student practicing a piano piece and then discuss it together. The residence also had a library and a large sitting room that I was free to use while the students were away on vacation.

Each week I attended a seminar held in Penrose's office. Penrose would sit in a chair that he tilted back until it rested against the blackboard behind him. At that time he was working on what are known as twistors. It was a theory he hoped would embrace space, time and the forces of nature. In short, an attempt at the unification of relativity and quantum theory. His seminars were a brilliant tour de force. I was aware of a person thinking on his feet and making new advances. He had the ability to discuss objects in many dimensions in what seemed to me a very visual way. One day someone brought in an article on the latest theory about the fine structure constant, one of the great mysteries of the quantum world. Penrose immediately recognized that it related to the intersection of spheres and light cones in higher dimensional spaces.

Dave Schrum was also in London taking his postdoctoral year. It was natural that he should do this with David Bohm, since his thesis had involved an application of Bohm's plasma theory to a metal surface. By coincidence Bohm was in the physics department at the same Birkbeck College. I had never met Bohm but many years earlier I had heard him speak on the radio. His discussion of an alternative to quantum theory had impressed me at the time. On the other hand I thought of Bohm as belonging to the past and Penrose as representing the future.

One day I walked over to the graduate room of the physics department to talk to Schrum. A heated discussion was in progress. One of the students was denying the importance of the absolute. His opponent, a man in his fifties, kept pressing the student in a Socratic way–eventually getting him to assert that there could be no statement that was absolutely true. "And is that statement itself absolute?" the older man asked.

I simply had to talk to this figure and followed him out of the room saying "I have to talk to you," but adding, "we must talk freely and openly." The man was David Bohm and several times a week I'd go to his office around four in the afternoon and we'd talk into the early evening when I would walk him to Goodge Street underground station where he took the train home to Edgware.

In our early discussions we looked into the foundations of quantum theory. Bohm pointed out that a number of interesting tensions existed in those early days–for example between Heisenberg's quantum mechanics and Schrödinger's wave mechanics. He felt that these tensions were deeply significant. The error had been in attempting to resolve them too quickly in order to establish a single orthodox interpretation. When things are left open and in tension, with no attempt at resolution, Bohm felt that the mind becomes filled with energy and is more acute. Instead that early enquiry had been dissipated and the deeper arguments closed off.

Niels Bohr in Copenhagen had been the major force in seeking a unification of quantum theory and so we discussed Bohr's writings. Although Bohm himself was a maverick who rejected Bohr's orthodox interpretation of quantum theory, he also had the deepest respect for Bohr and would not allow Bohr's ideas to be criticized in a loose way. It was like one of those marriages in which husband and wife always seem to be at loggerheads yet when an outsider criticizes one of them the couple close ranks and go on the attack together.

Those conversations with Bohm convinced me that few people really understood the subtleties of Bohr's philosophy. Indeed few physicists ever bothered to understand quantum theory at a deep level, or why such tensions had existed. As Bohm's long-term colleague, Basil Hiley, put it, people come to praise Bohr and decry Einstein (old classical school) but end up ignoring Bohr and thinking like Einstein.

In particular, we discussed Bohr's views on language and his remark that, when it came to a discussion of the nature of quantum reality, "We are suspended in language such that we don't know which way is up and which is down." Language became another focus of interest and therefore becomes the subject of the next essay.

But my year in England was not confined to physics alone. Taking a sabbatical gave me room to breathe. I visited museums and art galleries and haunted libraries. I went regularly to the theater and concerts and bought a season ticket to the Proms. At Goldsmith's College I took a course in electronic music composition with a composer who had collaborated with the Italian composer Luciano Berio and the singer Cathy Barberian.

And there was something more; a chance to visit Carl Jung in depth. Some years ago I had watched a television interview with Jung. In a BBC series called "Face to Face," John Freeman interviewed some of the leading thinkers and figures of the time. In his interview with Jung, the psychologist recalled that when he was a young doctor he had noticed a patient staring out of the window and moving his head. When questioned, the man said that he was looking at the sun which had a penis and that a wind came from the sun. Years later, when researching the Roman cult of Mithras, Jung came across a similar image. Why, he asked, should a modern Swiss have an identical image to that from ancient Rome? The answer, he felt, lay in his discovery of the collective unconscious–that area of the mind beyond the personal unconscious shared by all humanity and given structure by the archetypes. What Jung was saying spoke to the way I also experienced the world. I too had had intimations of an area of the mind that lies outside the confines of space and time and felt that deep down we come into direct contact with what is shared by all of us.

Over the winter, when the students had left college for their Christmas vacation, I would take books and sit in front of the fire in the large sitting room. At that time the Canadian dollar was high against the pound and so I could choose a bottle of good wine to drink while I read. Over this period I read Jung and the *I Ching* as well as books by Jung's students and followers. It was a quiet and peaceful time and new ideas were beginning to form. Ideas that would bear fruit several years later.

LANGUAGE AND SCIENCE

Excursion IV

Language has always been an abiding interest for me. Maybe it was my roots in Liverpool, a melting pot of English, Irish and Welsh and, being a seaport, several other nationalities as well. It was not only the home to the Beatles but also to a number of Britain's leading comedians. Language in Liverpool (specifically the dialect known as "scouse") has always been used as a humorous weapon to deflate the pretensions of others. Two of my friends from teenage days became linguists. David Crystal is author of several books on linguistics including the *Cambridge Encyclopedia of Language* and Alan "Clem" Ford specializes in indigenous languages of North America.

But why should language be of interest to a scientist? I was always struck by the fact that, around the same time period, both the philosopher Ludwig Wittgenstein and the physicist Niels Bohr were saying profound things about language. The remark, "We are suspended in language so that we don't know which way is up and which is down," could have been uttered by Wittgenstein during one of his lectures at Cambridge but is in fact Bohr's. Wittgenstein's initial aim had been to understand how we could say anything at all about the world. The important clue came when reading about a court case involving a traffic accident in which a model of the road with toy cars was produced. Wittgenstein realized that it was not just a matter of the toy cars corresponding to real cars but rather that the arrangement, the relationship of the cars to each other and to the road, corresponded to the arrangement of events of the accident in the external world.

In a similar way, he reasoned, the relationship of words in sentences and sentences to each other corresponds to the relationship of facts in the world. In this "picture theory" of language it becomes possible to set a boundary around the sorts of things we can say for certain about the world—all the rest being the province of poetry and literature. This was his seminal work, completed when the Italians held him a prisoner of war during the 1914-18 war. After that he gave up philosophy for a number of years until a meeting with an Italian economist caused him to make a radical revision of his philosophy.

While explaining his picture theory the Italian replied with that sweeping gesture from the chin that expresses contempt, "What does that correspond to?" he asked. Wittgenstein realized that this was a totally clear form of communication that corresponded to nothing in the world. He returned to Cambridge and used his seminars and lectures as laboratories in which to investigate the ways language really works. Clearly his earlier approach had been flawed. One can't make a boundary around language in this way. People employ words in a variety of ways even when speaking around the same topic. People will use words like "freedom," "truth," "ethics," and "consciousness" in very different ways as they debate an issue. "Don't ask what the word means," Wittgenstein said, "ask how it is used."

Take for example the word "game." It is used to describe a large number of human activities from chess to baseball, from children playing with a doll to a person playing solitaire. But is a crossword puzzle a game? Is doing mathematics a game? Try as you may you will never find one definition that embraces everything that is a game and excludes all activities that look similar but are not. In other words the familiar western way of gathering things into categories of thought is limited and can lead to confusion. Better to use the notion of family resemblances–there is no family "face" but some members may have similar eyes but different noses, while others have the same noses but different eyes. By gathering all these links together we begin to recognize the different members of a family.

It's the same with words in a philosophical argument–people believe they are talking about the same thing but they are making subtly different assumptions. For this reason, Wittgenstein, argued, maybe the Great Problems of Philosophy are no more than pseudo-problems brought about by a lack of attention to language. If you don't believe this then just ask a group of people to discuss the nature of consciousness together!

Wittgenstein compared philosophy to a man who goes into a room and feels trapped. He tries in vain to get out of the window or up the chimney never realizing that the door behind him is still open.

That we are suspended in language is the essence of Wittgenstein's work but it also emerged through the discussions in Copenhagen in which physicists were engaged. Bohr, Pauli and Heisenberg asked about the meaning of quantum theory. Heisenberg had once said, "If you want to understand the theory then look at the mathematics" but Bohr argued that when scientists write equations on the blackboard they have to discuss what they mean and how the various symbols are to be interpreted. This is where the problem arises, for when scientists discuss ideas they do so in what Bohr called "ordinary language." That is, in the language we all speak–with the addition of some technical terms.

Now this language is human-scaled and human-oriented. It evolved within a group of beings of a certain height, living on a planet with a certain gravitational force and going about the business of hunting, eating and making shelters. In other words, the physicality of life is deeply ingrained in language. Notions of space, time and causality are inextricably entwined in the language we speak. So when we try to speak about processes at the atomic level we inevitably and subconsciously import all sorts of ideas about duration, position, location, independent existence, intrinsic properties, forces, interactions and so on. We simply can't help this, and since these concepts are not really appropriate at the quantum scale of things, we find that we are contaminating what we want to speak about–we are truly suspended in language so that we cannot orient ourselves or escape this most basic of human conditions.

This, for Bohr, put a barrier on what can be said about the quantum world. The French physicist and philosopher, Bernard d'Espagnat, spoke of that world as being a "veiled reality" which implies that while we can never know the true face of reality below the atom it nevertheless exists. Bohr went much further. How far he went is difficult to discern because his writing is often hard to follow. He often said that the opposite of truth is falsehood. But the opposite of a great truth is another great truth. Thus when he had written a sentence in one of his papers he would try to contradict it with the next sentence!

At times Bohr seems to be saying that we have reached a limit as to what can be said and that to continue to ask about "quantum reality" would only lead us into confusion. At other times he seems to be saying that even the term "quantum reality" or "underlying reality" makes no sense and maybe doesn't even exist.

Although David Bohm disagreed with the interpretation of quantum theory worked out by Bohr, Pauli, Heisenberg and others in Copenhagen, he had always had great respect for Bohr's rigor of mind. His own approach to language was subtly different and left, he hoped, room for continued communication about the quantum domain.

Bohm pointed to the subject-predicate nature of many languages. We have a subject and an object linked by a verb. "The cat chases the mouse." We begin with two nouns, each have independently existing properties, and then link them together via some sort of action–the verb. This is analogous to what happens in the world of classical physics where independent objects interact by physical forces.

But the quantum world is holistic, Bohm argued. Its essence is not built out of independent elements like some tinker toy; rather all is process and movement. In fact Bohm referred to this as the holomovement–the movement of the whole.

So why not adopt a language that reflects this process-like nature of the quantum world, he asked, a language that is based in verbs and in which nouns emerge out of verbs just as objects at the quantum level could be thought of as approximations arising out of underlying quantum processes? He called this language the rheomode (the flowing mode).

Bohm published this idea as part of his seminal book *Wholeness and the Implicate Order*. On his visits to Brockwood Park–a school founded by Jiddu Krishnamurti where Bohm was a trustee–he would attempt to engage the staff and students in discussions using the rheomode. The reports I had were that the experiment did not go too well; indeed people began to use the "verbs" as nouns.

There was no real interest in Bohm's experiment on the part of linguists. They would probably have warned him of the difficulties in creating an artificial language. In addition, the theories of Noam Chomsky were in fashion at the time, in which particular human languages are pictured as only the surface structure that overlies the deeper linguistic structures common to all humankind. For a time Chomsky spelled the death to the Whorf-Sapir hypothesis which was more appealing to Bohm.

What was this hypothesis? Benjamin Lee Whorf was not a professional linguist but had studied the Hopi language and reflected on the way it classified the world. He argued that there is a deep connection between the way a particular language works and the world-view of its speakers. I'm afraid that Whorf is largely misunderstood or misrepresented as one often finds statements to the effect that "language determines the way we see the world," which was not what Whorf intended. By demolishing that rather strong statement people then think they have demolished Whorf.

It is certainly true that all professions adopt a special "language," in the sense of a series of technical terms that enable them to deal with the world with much greater discrimination. Doctors must learn the names of all the bones in the foot, for example. Faced with a skeleton I and a doctor would see the same foot, yet the doctor would be far more aware of subtle distinctions and relationships than I would because he has been given the fine tool of language. Something similar applies to lawyers, ships' captains, biologists and theologians. Learning a specialized language helps us to communicate with greater precision and to share a refined perception of the world. In turn the way we deal with that world leads to further refinements and developments of that language.

This is probably what Bohm was pointing towards. If we can develop a new language and begin to communicate about process in general, and in particular to processes at the level of the quantum, then we can extend our ability to communicate and to think about the quantum world.

The story does not end here for there is one more step to be made and this involves a journey to the land of the Blackfoot in Alberta and Montana.

Radio days

Chapter 5

My discussions with Bohm ranged over science, language, and the role of mathematics. When it came to the unification of quantum theory and relativity Bohm argued that new ideas or new mathematics were not enough. What was required was a radically new order in physics. Then, one evening, it suddenly struck me that science was only the outer aspect of what we were talking about. I immediately phoned Bohm and said, "What we were really discussing is consciousness and the nature of the human mind." Bohm said, "Come and see me tomorrow." From now on our conversations entered a new field–the nature of human consciousness, perception and the possible limitations of consciousness and its transformation. At that time I had not known that Bohm had been having long discussions with Jiddu Krishnamurti.

It was about this time that I should have been moving on to the second half of my sabbatical. Since officially I was still supposed to be working on solid-state physics at the National Research Council of Canada, I was pushing my luck in spending all that time with Bohm and Penrose on what were highly speculative ideas. By way of compensation, I had arranged to spend the next six months in a solid-state group run by a very respected theoretician. Some weeks before I was due to transfer out of London the head of the group invited me for dinner where I was subjected to a fatherly chat. I was warned about Bohm. I was still a young researcher, he said, with many years of good work ahead of me. I should build a strong reputation in an orthodox field. But, by associating myself so openly with Bohm, I would become suspect within the scientific community. Bohm's views were not well grounded, he said. Many years ago Bohm had proposed a theory that had been proved to be incorrect. His scholarly work on plasmas had been brilliant but it was best if I dissociate myself from him. I didn't take the advice and decided to spend the full year at Birkbeck with Bohm and Penrose.

Ironically that story of an incorrect theory continues to be repeated in the scientific community. While the full background can be found in my biography of Bohm, *Infinite Potential: The Life and Times of David Bohm*, the essence of the story is worth repeating here for the light it throws on the sociology of science.

While at Princeton after the war, Bohm was working on an alternative approach to quantum theory called "hidden variables." This was also the period of McCarthy's anti-communist witch-hunt. Bohm himself was questioned and, following his refusal to give names of those suspected of having communist sympathies, he was arrested for contempt of Congress. He was acquitted at the trial, nevertheless the authorities of Princeton University forbade him to set foot on the campus. As far as they were concerned Bohm had become a tainted figure. As a result, Bohm accepted a position in Brazil. Soon after his arrival in that country, the US consul confiscated his American passport.

Bohm was out of the US but his theory remained and Oppenheimer called a seminar to discuss hidden variables. In those days it was politically expedient to distance oneself from suspect characters. Therefore, although this was a scientific meeting, Bohm's former colleagues publicly denounced him as being "a fellow traveler" and doing "Trotskyite physics." Oppenheimer believed that he too would come under investigation and was also willing to discredit Bohm. (Earlier he had told investigators that Bohm was "politically suspect.") But to discredit Bohm first it would be necessary to demolish his hidden variable theory. Yet, try as they could, the assembled physicists could not find a flaw in Bohm's paper. In the end Oppenheimer announced, "If we can't disprove Bohm we must all agree to ignore him." The word was out!

Even today many of the older generation of physicists will tell you that Bohm's approach to quantum theory, even the work he did in the years leading up to his death, is incorrect. In most cases it turns out that they haven't even read his papers and, when pressed as to the nature of the error in Bohm's approach, they will say that they don't actually know, but they do "know" that Bohm is wrong. Fortunately that attitude is now changing. As Bohm himself said, "I won't convince people now but the next generation may take up my ideas." Indeed Bohm's approach, under the title of "The Causal Interpretation" can now be found in textbooks.

Eventually my sabbatical year came to the end and I returned to Canada. There I began a program of research to look into the foundations of quantum theory. In particular I had become interested in what is known as "the collapse of the wave function"–the way in which something definite emerges from a series of probabilities. To this end I was trying to make a connection between thermodynamics and quantum theory and also to look at non-unitary operators that would allow for irreversibility in a quantum measurement. Looking back I can see I had been on the right track but I have only published one or two papers on the subject. I still have a draft of another written twenty-five years ago which I never got round to revising. I'd also played around with these ideas in connection with black holes and looked at the possibility of matter-energy escaping from the event horizon. In this case Stephen Hawking published the seminal paper–but at least it was nice to think my intuitions had pushed me in the right direction.

In addition to a new direction for research there were other

London experiences that I intended to pursue back in Canada. One thing that had been revived in me by my visit to London was the power of radio to produce high quality documentaries. In the early 1970s the BBC Third Programme was still a hive of intellectual stimulation, for in those days the media had not yet been "dumbed down." To this end I approached the Canadian Broadcasting Corporation with the idea of a program on science.

This was to be my first meeting with Paul Buckley, a scientist turned radio producer, and the start of a creative relationship. Incidentally Paul visited me here in Pari just as I was about to write this chapter and so the recollections of our work together have found its way into this writing. Paul came down to Ottawa one Thursday and said he would be happy to commission a fifty-five-minute script. I asked him how many weeks I had and he replied, "Two days." The program was to be recorded on Sunday.

I drove home and went to bed—where much of my best work is done. I lay there and began to think about what I wanted to do. I had always loved Dylan Thomas' radio play *Under Milk Wood*, subtitled "a play for voices." And so too, voices came to me, voices talking in counterpoint about ideas in modern physics, others representing "the critical voice of hard-nosed science." I also knew how I wanted the program to begin and to end, for it formed a circle. It started with a canon from Bach's *Musical Offering* and ended with the same piece transcribed by the twentieth century composer Anton von Webern.

My next surprise occurred when Paul arrived on Sunday morning. He read over the script and announced, "Find two friends and bring your children, we'll all record it together." Normally a piece for six voices would be recorded on separate tracks and later mixed. Instead Paul wanted to try something more immediate and arranged microphones around the table. He then conducted us while we read and moved our heads towards and away from the microphones.

A few more scripted programs followed and then came a remarkable series of twenty one-hour programs called "Physics and Beyond" for the CBC "Ideas" series. For these Paul Buckley and I traveled in Europe and the USA to interview such people as Werner Heisenberg, Paul Dirac, Ilya Prigogine, Roger Penrose, David Bohm, Abus Salam and many others of the leading figures who had created modern physics. I well remember the interview with Dirac. We had traveled to Florida and at first Dirac refused to speak to us, "I don't speak to reporters," he said. However his wife (referred to by Dirac as "Wigner's sister") suggested we simply go round to where they were staying and she would persuade him to speak for a few minutes.

We arrived and the engineer set up the microphones. We first asked Dirac if he would comment on something. "No," came the reply. He was then asked if he would read the opening preface of his book on quantum theory. "No, if people want to know about this they can buy the book and read it."

Then it hit me, and I asked him about beauty in physics. Dirac lit up and began to speak with passion. When the tape ran out he seemed rather disappointed that we couldn't continue with the interview.

There was one scientist we never did interview, Joachim Fruitman. I invented him one afternoon during our tour of Europe. Paul was about to fly to Sweden to interview Abus Salam and I was going to London to interview Penrose and Bohm. Before each interview I would brief Paul, as producer. But, by now, with so many interviews the real scientists were becoming a little surreal; that's where Fruitman came in. He had been a member of the Vienna Circle before an embarrassing incident involving Carl Popper had occurred. I even found a photo of Fruitman—it was of the Vienna circle with a couple of members out of focus.

In the previous Diversion we have seen how Bohr stressed that "we are suspended in language," and when we try to speak about quantum reality we import all manner of linguistic assumptions.

Therefore, as with Wittgenstein, it was important to be very attentive to language. Fruitman had gone one step beyond into diction. In order to discuss quantum theory, he had written, it was necessary to speak clearly and with good pronunciation. Otherwise we would not understand the argument. For a time at least I managed to persuade Paul that such a character existed and later we slipped in occasional references to him in the scripts.

With the recordings completed I went to Toronto where they were to be broadcast every evening Monday to Friday over a month. This meant having a program ready to be broadcast by the evening. Paul edited the interviews throughout the night and first thing in the morning he would tell me to write "a five-minute introduction to the program, then a two-minute intro for Wheeler, you'll also have four minutes to explain the theory of relativity and a one-minute to wrap up at the end." While I worked on these, Paul would be starting on the next day's programs. In turn my scripts had to be ready by the afternoon so that the announcer's part could be recorded and spliced into the tape.

I'd call all of this "learning on the job." I suppose the alternative is to take a script-writing course but far more exciting is to be told, "Write me seven minutes on x and have it ready in two hours from now."

We did one more series—interviews at a conference of scientists and Krishnamurti. But in this case Paul didn't ask me to write any scripts. He took me into the studio at night and turned out all the lights. "Sit and listen," he said, "and when the red light comes on just speak and continue speaking until the light goes out."

It was a curious experience. It was late at night and I was tired. I'd listen in the dark to the voice of Krishnamurti, Maurice Wilkins, David Bohm or Fritjof Capra and then, suddenly, the voice would stop and I would find myself talking, commenting, exploring. And that was the way those five programs were made.

But things don't go on forever. Those two or three years saw some of the most creative radio documentaries made by a handful of producers. It was also the period when the great Canadian pianist, Glenn Gould, used the same studio to make his documentaries with voices in counterpoint, such as *Idea of North.* In fact we used the same technician, Lorne Tulk, who, over a beer, would tell us anecdotes about Gould.

Then policy changed, the executive producer left and so did several other producers including Paul. For a time radio was closed to me. But later I was to write another documentary and several radio plays. Radio will always be close to my heart.

SCHRÖDINGER'S CAT OR THE QUANTUM MEASUREMENT PROBLEM

Excursion V

One of the great dilemmas facing quantum theory dates back to its earliest days and is often associated with the name of Erwin Schrödinger. In the world of classical physics a falling stone, the baseball from a pitcher's hand, or a comet approaching the solar system, all have definite paths through space. Given data on the position and the speed (technically the momentum) of an object and the forces acting on it, physics can tell us exactly where it will be at any future moment in time. In other words, corresponding to each specific situation there will be a unique solution.

This is not the case in quantum theory because there can be many possible solutions to any given situation–in fact there can be an infinite number of them. The description of a moving body in the classical world is given by a path or trajectory in space, whereas in quantum theory (specifically in what is known as Hilbert space) the description looks more like a series of arrows pointing in different directions. Each arrow represents one particular solution and, moreover, any combination of arrows is allowed.

Since that may sound too abstract let's go to the paradox expressed by Schrödinger. It involves putting a cat in a box with a radioactive isotope and a jar of cyanide. Here the reader should note that Schrödinger was proposing what is called a *gedanken* experiment, i.e. one that is technically possible but is performed only in the imagination. No real cats are involved! Place a Geiger counter next to the radioactive substance. If it disintegrates, the counter clicks and triggers a hammer that smashes the flask of cyanide and the cat dies. If it does not then the cat lives. Now put the cat in the box, close the lid and plan to open it again after sixty minutes. This is where the paradox arises.

Disintegration of a radioactive atom is a matter of pure chance. Suppose there is a 50:50 chance that this will happen within the next hour. Quantum theory tells us that there are two possible solutions–disintegrated and non-disintegrated. But the theory also allows us to combine these two solutions in any way we want. Therefore just before we open the box quantum theory argues that all possible solutions exist. That is, inside is not only a live cat and a dead cat, but also a cat that is 50% alive and 50% dead, a cat that is 99% alive and 1% dead and so on. However the moment we open the box, the moment we observe the system, we see either a dead cat or a live cat.

Put another way, the wave function is the most complete description possible of a quantum system and this wave function involves all possible combinations of solutions–of live and dead cats. Yet the moment the box is opened, the moment any quantum measurement is made, all these possibilities collapse into one actuality. This is known as "the collapse of the wave function." A second before the box is opened there are an infinite number of possibilities of live and dead cats. A second later there is only one outcome for the wave function has "collapsed."

This paradox was presented by Schrödinger and had to be faced by Bohr, Heisenberg, Einstein, Wigner and all who came after them. Each tried a particular way out. Heisenberg, for example, took a Platonic view of the matter. These particular solutions given by the Schrödinger equation were "potentialities," while what was observed was an "actuality." The "potentialities" existed in some sort of Platonic world of ideas while the result of observation existed in our material world.

Eugene Wigner tried another tack. For him it was human consciousness that did the trick of collapsing the wave function. But even here another paradox arises. The human observer only sees a single result—a live cat or a dead cat. But how do we know if these are not perhaps two possible states of consciousness that co-exist in the observer? This means that the observer has superposed states of consciousness that can only be collapsed by a second observer who observes the first…and so on ad infinitum.

There were even more bizarre solutions one of which was the hypothesis of infinite worlds. When the box is opened each potential solution is actually realized, but each in a different universe. In other words at every measurement the universe split with each different universe containing one of the solutions. To my mind this is the most absurd proposal I have ever come across, yet many scientists take it quite seriously.

This collapse of the wave function was one of the problems I was looking at when I returned from London. I had become interested in the connection between thermodynamics and quantum theory. I'd also been working on the issue of thermodynamics and black holes. As regards quantum theory it was clear to me that a quantum system coupled to a larger-scale thermodynamic system (such as a cat), but isolated from the world in a box, cannot exist in a superposed state. Rather its Hilbert space will become partitioned so that an actual solution can be found in only one of these subspaces. This would mean that while a degree of uncertainty would remain, nevertheless larger quantum systems would have definite properties. While a live cat may die, it is a thermodynamic impossibility that a dead cat, sealed in a box, will come to life.

This touches on another issue, that of reversibility. We know that time's arrow moves in only one direction in our world–from past to future. However the laws of physics are always time symmetric. Flick a switch and a room fills with light–but physics also allows for the reverse solution–that light implodes from all corners of the room into the bulb. This sounds absurd but the equations of physics allow for this. Physicists have two options. One is simply to reject one set of solutions as being impossible and unphysical. The other is to assume that all the laws of physics are created, or given to us, in totally symmetric ways. That means that the universe is free to go in one direction or another, but that at the first instants of creation a choice was made. The choice may be arbitrary but once it has been made there is no going back and the universe and all its processes move in one direction only. This is known as "symmetry breaking." It tells us that while nature's laws are highly symmetric, the actual physical outcomes have a much lower symmetry and are symmetry-broken. In this case it means that all processes move from present into the future rather than the reverse–or both!

The equations of quantum theory are time-symmetric–moving equally from future to past as from past to future. But what if quantum theory is also symmetry-broken? What if processes can only go in one direction? Conventional quantum theory uses what are termed "unitary operators," i.e. they can take a quantum system from one state of being to another. In turn all these operations are totally reversible. My own approach was to work with non-unitary operators–a quantum system can go from A to B, but not from B to A. In this way a definite arrow of time is introduced and outcomes are definite. One can go from a live to a dead cat but not vice versa. Before the box is opened the cat is definitively alive or dead!

RE-ENCOUNTERING CARL JUNG

Chapter 6

O ur theoretical group had a small budget and tradition had it that each year one member of the group should choose how to spend the money by inviting visitors for a week or a month at a time. Following my sabbatical year in London it was my turn. My plan was to have some highly creative thinkers drop in over the summer to stimulate discussion. These included theoretical physicists such as David Finkelstein, Elliott Lieb, David Bohm and Ilya Prigogine (who later was awarded the Nobel Prize) as well as theoretical biologists Howard Pattee and Robert Rosen. In addition, I asked a few artists to engage in dialogue with the group of theoreticians. I also planned to invite the American composer, John Cage, to talk about chance.

Bohm himself came for two months and gave a series of seminars that were well attended by those outside the National Research Council. I felt that it was possible to push our group to a new level. I was not interested in the dull and mediocre. We should be engaged in the very latest ideas. At the time I didn't see the danger signals–that not everyone would share my point of view. Many people are content doing what they have always done and resent their calm waters being stirred.

I should have been politically more sophisticated and have recalled that fatherly talk I had been given in England! While I'd been away a Canadian Royal Commission had been looking at scientific research across Canada. It had defined a series of national objectives and adopted a bizarre form of classification. Work directly focused on one of these objectives was termed "mission-oriented research" and was clearly "a good thing." What the commissioners had not realized was that this allowed the mediocre in science, but the sophisticated in politics, to simply rewrite their current research projects to give the appearance of being specifically concerned with one of the national objectives. They received funding support and then went on doing what they had always been doing.

Projects not directly related to practical advances of the national objectives were termed "curiosity-oriented." At one time such work had been highly regarded as "pure research" and many of the advances in technology had emerged out of pure research. But now purity had been downgraded to mere curiosity. And we all know that curiosity killed the cat! Thus at the height of Bohm's visit I was told that I had invited a man who was "trouble from start to finish" and that what I was doing was far too speculative to be justified under the new policy. It would be better if I left the group or transferred to another division.

After buying two more years of time, I left NRC. On the one hand it meant leaving the security of a job and a salary for the great unknown. But in so many other ways it was an enormous relief to escape from the confines of the National Research Council; after all I had already been leaving on a daily basis as I climbed through my office window and went to sit and think beside the waterfall. I now felt totally free to do exactly what I wanted to do. In a burst of fun I took all my severance pay and spent it on making a film, *Memories*.

For a number of years I had had an interest in film as a medium, particularly in the "language" of film and the way images run together in a montage. Maybe this language was an important clue to our own pre-verbal processing of the world. Watching a film certainly was "dreaming in the dark." I also felt that the early directors, through the use of editing and cutting from long shot into close up, had discovered the way the eye-brain works several decades before the psychologists.

The film I made was of a photographer and his connection to the past through an image he has taken. I used a number of local actors and technicians who worked without pay. We rehearsed each scene carefully. Since we couldn't afford to buy very much black and white 16mm film stock, we limited ourselves to one or two takes of each scene. As to sound, that was recorded independently and added at the editing stage–takes with live sound are too often spoiled by extraneous noises. I had a young composer create part of an electronic score; a local jazz group supplied the rest.

I had assumed that working with actors and a crew would have been the most exciting and creative part of filmmaking. I was therefore surprised when I moved to the Steenbeck editing bed. This enables you to run a film on a small screen at anything from fast forward, through normal speed and down to a single frame-by-frame sequence. In this way different takes and parts of a take can be spliced together or dissolved one into the other. Initially this editing process involved logical decisions to do with unfolding the story of the film. But once the various scenes had been arranged in sequence the more serious side of editing took place. This was about establishing the pace, the visual rhythms of the film, and selecting the way various physical movements fit together according to how the eye scans the screen and moves from scene to scene, as well as the frame-by-frame relationships of light, form and shape.

Taken at the intellectual, analytic level this task would seem to be enormously complicated, but after a few hours I found that my hands were making rapid decisions about where to cut and splice, even to the point of overruling the rational mind. It was as if the movements and relationships of the film had become internalized in muscular reflexes; the film had become feelings in the stomach, subtle movements and a symphony of sensations. Again I was discovering how much of the creative process takes place within the body itself and outside the range of the conscious mind.

Related sensations were created in me some time later when I viewed the completed piece in a cinema. It had its debut at the local repertory cinema as the warm-up to *The Rocky Horror Picture Show*! I would like to have made more films but simply didn't have the money and I was not the type of person who could comfortably go knocking on doors with proposals in my hand. Today with a digital camera and computer editing software it would be so much easier and cheaper.

I very much enjoyed visits to the repertory cinema that had agreed to premiere my film for it also featured films by Fellini, Bergman, Antonioni, Godard and Buñuel. Fellini remains my favorite director and for me *8½* is one of the greatest films ever made. I once had a dream about Fellini. We were standing together at the rail of a ferryboat looking towards the shore. I said to Fellini that when I was a boy there was sand like that beside the River Mersey in Liverpool. Fellini also came from a seaside town, Rimini. He turned to me and said, "When I was a boy there were ibexes." In another dream Fellini was directing a great march that began with people followed by animals, right back to dinosaurs and even rocks.

I was also excited by Ken Russell and his use of the image. Those who know Russell's name probably associate him with extravagant feature films such as *The Music Lovers* and *Lisztomania* but I also knew his early work for the BBC during the 1950s and '60s when he produced remarkable documentaries on Debussy, Bartók, Delius, Elgar and Strauss as well as the poet Rossetti and the dancer Isadora Duncan. One time Russell came to Ottawa for a retrospective of his films. I met him at a reception and was probably the only person present who knew of his early work. We talked together for two hours and he explained how he would love to film Virginia's Woolf's *To the Lighthouse*. This was a proj-ect that never materialized for him.

Recently I watched *Memories* again and noticed something quite interesting. A close-up of two hands meeting was virtually identical to a close-up in Ken Russell's film *Delius* and the gesture of a woman touching her hair mirrored Claudia Cardinale's in Fellini's *8½*. I was struck by the way a visual image, seen only once in the case of *Delius* and that ten years earlier, was able to be captured and remain in the memory is such a vivid way.

It was around this time my father died. My mother was natu-rally very distressed so her sister, Auntie Hilda, came to stay in the house with her. On the night after the funeral my aunt began to have severe chest pains and several hours later died of a heart attack. My mother tried to carry on by herself but the area in which she lived had declined and petty crime was on the rise.

Now it was necessary to bring my mother back to Canada to live with us, but first I had to spend some time settling the fam-ily affairs. One day I looked in at the new library that my father, first as chair of the library committee and then as town mayor had worked hard to have built. There was a photograph of him in the entrance hall. While walking around someone called me over and said he had been present at my father's death. "It was the night of the general election," he said. "Your father was very excited and then the news came. The Conservatives were win-ning; Mrs. Thatcher would be prime minister. Your father said, 'Put the kettle on and let's have a cup of tea together. This is the happiest day of my life.' I turned to put on the kettle and heard a thump. Your father had fallen off his chair and was dead." And so my father had died happy, a good way to go but looking back I cannot ignore the irony of all that the age of Mrs. Thatcher was to bring to Britain.

Most of my mother's life had been spent as a professional invalid–albeit one who lived to see the age of ninety. She was always sickly, unable to go out, suffering from headaches and various weaknesses. Somewhat in the manner of a character in Proust she had to remain for periods of time in a darkened bedroom with her eyes closed. Once, when a little boy, she even asked me to fetch a pencil and paper so she could write down her "last thoughts." At times she was mysteriously taken to hospital in the night. Yet one by one the doctors who had treated her for her many ailments died before her and she lived on. Only when she played the piano did true passion emerge.

She read a great deal but only religious tracts or books of self-improvement. She would not pick up a work of fiction for, in her youth, she had once read a novel but then become "painfully disillusioned" by an event in real life. It is hard for me to imagine the world in which my mother, as invalid, existed. Many years later when she was in her eighties and living with us there happened to be a power cut. We lit candles and I went to my mother's room to let her know everything was fine and that it was just a temporary black-out. "Oh," she said, "I thought I'd suddenly gone blind." On another occasion around that same period she was convinced she had cancer of the esophagus and went for tests at the local hospital. Later, in the specialist's office, she was assured that nothing was wrong with her. As I walked her to the car she appeared very shaken. "I'll never get over the shock of finding I don't have cancer," she told me.

She lived with us for seventeen years from the time of my father's death. Towards the end of her life she developed a friend, "the girl." The "girl" lived on the other side of the dresser mirror in her bedroom and the two of them would carry on long conversations together. At times my mother would try to climb behind the mirror in order to get closer to her. Their meetings together continued in a cordial fashion for a number of months until my mother discovered that the "girl" was in the habit of taking exactly the same medication as she herself–presumably the girl had stolen it while my mother was out of the room. The girl also had the annoying habit of dressing in clothes identical to my mother's. At first my mother tried to fool her by hiding while she dressed, but as soon as she walked towards the dresser she would discover that the girl had exactly anticipated her choice. However hard she tried she could never fool the girl.

Nevertheless the girl remained an important factor in my mother's life. My mother would often excuse herself from the table because the girl needed her. Finally my mother slipped and fell very early one morning while "going to school." She broke her hip and a few days later she died. She is buried in the tiny cemetery here in Pari.

Those years outside the confines of the National Research Council were a time of great experimentation. After the film came scripts for a number of radio plays, some of which I directed. I even wrote plays for the stage and tried my hand at theater directing. I love working with people in a collaborative way and directing proved an enjoyable break from the business of writing that can sometimes be very solitary. But, of course, bills had to be paid. So I taught a couple of courses at Carleton University in Ottawa and became a consultant for the Science Council of Canada and also contributed to their Foresight Group–a think-tank on future social implications of science.

I also became a writer. This was in part to convey my own enthusiasms. It connected me to that part of my childhood in which I had made regular trips to the library in order to devour books. I was writing for people who were like me and who were interested in exploring ideas. I also wrote because I wanted to understand things myself. There is a maxim that if you really want to understand something you should either give a course of lectures on the subject or write a book about it. In the months leading up to a new book I would normally read a lot, getting ideas from books or something heard on the radio or read in a magazine. All of this catalyses me to think. A very good time to think is when listening to a boring lecture. The mind wanders, odd phrases intrude and suddenly you find yourself writing down a new idea. Out of this comes an overall concept of "the next book" and I would write a proposal for an editor.

During the actual writing of a book I try to avoid reading anything on a related topic. I don't really think it's about the fear of being influenced; maybe it is more related to the alchemical process that must be carried out behind closed doors. In a similar way the topic about which I am writing must, in a certain sense, be sealed off. The exception to this was my biography of David Bohm, which had to be based on research and interviews. However during the actual writing of that book I only went back to the source material in order to check a date or a quotation. Then when the book was complete I did a final round of checking to confirm I had not made any factual mistakes.

One of the first books I was to work on was about synchronicity, an idea of Carl Jung. The Canadian Jungian, Jean-François Vézina, has written about "the meetings that transform us" and compared such meetings to the transformative effects of a true synchronicity when inner and outer worlds connect. My own synchronistic meeting with Carl Jung, had not been in the flesh but, as I wrote in a previous chapter, through a BBC television interview. Now, as a writer, it was the time to come face to face with one of Jung's key ideas–synchronicity. If I were to understand synchronicity I would have to write a book about it. *Synchronicity: The Bridge between Matter and Mind* was published in 1987 and is still selling. It has been my most popular book. Since that time I have been asked to speak at Jung Institutes and conferences and have established friendships with a number of Jungian analysts. Now, as I write this autobiographical piece, I realize it is time for a further encounter this time not only with Jung but also with Wolfgang Pauli.

Pauli himself was one of the most outstanding physicists of his age. He had even published on the theory of relativity before leaving high school! Pauli was inspired by a vision of overarching symmetry in physics. On the basis of symmetry principles alone he had predicted the existence of the neutrino–a massless, charge-less particle that was not to be discovered until twenty-five years after Pauli's prediction. He was also responsible for the famous Pauli Exclusion Principle, which was also related to principles of symmetry and antisymmetry in nature. Pauli referred to these as "God and the Devil" which he struggled to reconcile.

Around the age of thirty he experienced a psychological cri-sis and consulted Carl Jung. During therapy, and for the rest of his life, the physicist experienced many remarkable dreams that convinced him that he should direct his energies to a marriage of physics and psychology, matter and psyche. Physics, Pauli ar-gued, must come to terms with the irrational in matter. And, just as Jung had shown that there is an objective side to the mind (the collective unconscious), so too physics should discover its subjec-tive side. Pauli also felt that soul had been banished from the world with the rise of science. Now it was time for a resurrection of soul in the world of matter.

What particularly interests me about Pauli is that his inner and his outer work were always in parallel. His outer work was devoted to a unified theory of physics while his inner world was that of dreams in which a series of figures "the Chinese woman," "the stranger" would appear to him with messages from the un-conscious. With Pauli it was a constant struggle to unify inner and outer, psyche and matter, physics and psychology. In some ways he identified with Kepler, one of the first of the modern scientists, yet in others with the alchemist Flood. Indeed, dis-turbed by what he saw as the increasing "will to power" amongst scientists in their desire to control nature, he pleaded that "we do science like the alchemists of old…for our own redemption." For Pauli science revealed the wholeness in nature that, in turn, may help us to understand the wholeness that lies within.

When I think of figures, such as Pauli and Bohm I feel that they were both sensing the edge of something new, that they were in a certain sense "witnesses." It is as if something is about to be born, that something is beginning to take form on the horizon. As to what that is we do not really know but some have the sense of its presence, of something that transcends the division between matter, psyche and spirit. That, I feel, will be the subject of my next book.

David's maternal great-grandparents, Francis and Anne Spratt, with their sons and daughters.
David's grandmother is seated at the front of the picture.

Taken at the diamond wedding of David's paternal grandparents. Cousin Ann, James Peat, Edith Peat and David.

Baby David with his train set.
The area behind is a rockery designed to hide the air raid shelter.

David and his mother in Auntie Hilda's garden.

Auntie Hilda in her nurse's uniform with a baby David.

David in his first school uniform. The twist of the head does not indicate "cuteness" but torticollis, a condition involving the muscles of the neck which was later corrected by surgery.

38 Queensway, Waterloo, Liverpool 22. The house where David grew up. His daughter Eleanor is standing on the wall.

Standing: Geoffrey Peat (David's father) and Uncle Tim.
Seated: Marjorie (David's mother), his grandmother and Auntie Hilda.

David, the schoolboy, posing as the young scientist.

David working on his first research project, monitoring a chemical reaction.

Snow on Fentiman
Ave, David's
Ottawa home.

The extended family
Back row: Alex, Marcel, Emma, Sarah, Matthew, David's mother.
Front row: Maureen, Jason, Eleanor.

Leroy Little Bear and his wife Amethyst First Rider.

David Bohm and
David Peat at
the Bailey Farms
Institute in New
York State.

David teaching at the Pari Center.

The Pari Center conference room.

Participants at a Pari Center conference on "The Future of Knowledge in the World of the Internet" standing on the steps of the Palazzo where the Center has its offices and conference room.

David's grandchildren who live in Pari: Chiara, Alessandro and James.

SYNCHRONICITY

Excursion VI

The psychologist Carl Jung introduced the notion of synchronicity to describe those striking and apparently inexplicable occurrences in which, for example, the contents of a dream are paralleled in a pattern of seemingly unconnected external events. In his writings they are variously described as "meaningful coincidences," "significantly related patterns of chance," and "an acausal connecting principle."

Take the two following examples related to me by an analyst. In one, a psychotic patient shouted that he was Jesus and that he was the creator and destroyer of light. At the same instant the light fixture in the room broke away from the ceiling and fell on the patient's head! In the second, a wife receives a significant dream at the same time as her husband, in analysis in a different country, experiences a crisis leading to a profound transformation. Jung himself gave the case of a female patient who was resistant to treatment. She was relating a highly significant dream in which a golden scarab appeared. At that moment Jung heard a tapping at his window and, on opening it, observed a golden scarab beetle fly into the room. For the patient involved it was "her scarab" from the dream. Up to that point she had resisted treatment but from that moment the therapy progressed.

Synchronicities can occur when people enter into times of crisis or change, when they are in love, engaged in highly creative work, or on the verge of a breakdown. These are moments when the boundaries of mind and matter are transcended and people escape from the normal hard and fast distinctions they make between inner/outer, subjective/objective, psyche/matter. It suggests that patterns exist which embrace both the mental and the physical worlds. Indeed, Jung invented another word, the psychoid, to describe a level that lies beyond matter and mind and contains them both. Another useful metaphor is that of the speculum or a mirror that reflects one world into another, yet belongs to neither.

Synchronicity suggests a possible liaison or bridge between two worlds. On the one hand we have the inner world of our direct experiences, of dreams and aspirations, of memories and visions. It is the world of love and loss, of poetry, art and music. It is also the world of spirituality and numinosity. And, on the other, the world of matter and energy, the domain of physics and chemistry, the world of black holes, galaxies, elementary particles and quantum fields. And so, in speaking of synchronicity, one asks if a bridge is possible between these worlds, between mind and body, between matter and spirit.

Or perhaps one should go further by asking if the very way the question has been posed already exposes a fundamental fragmentation within our thinking. Are there indeed two such different worlds? Or are there simply two sides to the one reality, two reflections in the one speculum, and two modes of experience? Is it perhaps the particular way of seeing and of thinking within our western society, indeed the reflection of the language we speak that causes us to speak in terms of two worlds and then to seek to erect a bridge between them?

A number of important questions underlie these speculations: Is the universe built out of what could be termed dead and indifferent matter? Are our lives no more than the result of chance processes? Is the cosmos devoid of all meaning? Or could it be that we inhabit a living universe, a universe that is filled with significance, a universe that is a home for humanity and, indeed, for all life? Are we, in effect, spectators or participators within the universe?

For me Jung's synchronicity is closely tied to the idea of *epiphany* explored by the Irish writer James Joyce. Each one of us will have experienced, at some point in our lives, a moment of manifestation in which the world, our thoughts and memories, indeed everything within and without us becomes integrated and charged in a numinous fashion. It is as if the things around us, the significance of what we are about to do and the pattern of our life becomes unified within a field of meaning, a meaning that is at one and the same time universal, yet highly specific to the details of our own particular history and character.

Probably the best-known example from Joyce's own work occurs at the end of his short story "The Dead" (from his collection of stories, *Dubliners*). Gabriel Conway, a man who appears divorced from his feelings, has been to a dinner during the Christmas season with family and old friends in Dublin. During the dinner his wife has expressed a desire to visit Galway. Back in their hotel room she becomes pensive and Gabriel presses her to reveal her thoughts. In the end she tells him she was thinking of the song a young man, Michael Furey, used to sing to her back in Galway. Gabriel becomes angry and suspects she is still in love with the man and that is why she wishes to return to Galway. But then she tells him that the young man is dead. He was of frail health and sang outside her window in the rain the night before she left. She learned that he had died shortly afterwards.

His wife begins to sob and then falls asleep, leaving Gabriel with his thoughts and more importantly with a new feeling that he recognizes as love. At that moment he hears a tapping on the window and realizes it is snowing. He knows that the snow is falling all over Ireland. It will be falling all over the central plain, on the River Shannon, and even on the churchyard where Michael Furey is buried. Gabriel feels his soul fainting and the snow "...faintly falling, like the descent of their last end, upon all the living and the dead." And so at this moment of epiphany the falling snow unites the living and the dead. Possibly it is at this moment that the reader asks if this event is taking place on January 6, the feast of the Epiphany.

Perhaps the most celebrated and deeply explored series of epiphanies occurs in Marcel Proust's *A la recherche du temps perdu* as, for example, in the first volume *Du côté de chez Swann* in which the narrator, bringing to his lips the teaspoon containing a fragment of a *petite Madeleine*, is overtaken with an extraordinary sense of pleasure and joy which then causes him to enquire into the origin of these intense feelings and associations.

I have introduced this idea of epiphany because, for me, it focuses upon what I feel to be the essence and the importance of a synchronicity–that sense of a unifying pattern of meaning, which brings together in a perfectly seamless way the unfolding movement of inner and outer events.

Epiphanies and synchronicities are concerned with the harmony and balance between inner and outer; between, on the one hand, the world of mind and spirit and, on the other, the world of matter, space, time and causality. On an individual basis, synchronicities may be experienced as patterns, pregnant with meaning, that spill over from the world of dreams, memories and visions into similar patterns of concrete physical events in the external, "objective" world.

But such experiences bring us face to face with an essential paradox, namely, what sort of connection could there be that lies outside all causality? Or, more specifically, what meaning can be given to the term *acausality* and by what manner does a pattern of very different and causally unconnected events unfold within the confines of space and time?

Despite the quantum revolution of the early decades of this century, we still live in a world of causality and the inevitable flow of time from past into present. Indeed, to a physicist, every event in the physical world is the end point of a causal chain involving *unitary transformations*; that is, the particular state of the present is totally determined as being a function of a state in the past. Likewise, the implications of the future are causally and completely contained within the present.

And so when we look from this perspective at a pattern of events in the physical world we seek the causal chains that link them. We look for the operation of the forces of physics, for transformations of energy and for the inevitable march of time. And, in doing so, we give little importance to the occurrence of related dreams, memories and visions.

If our classical physics denies the very nature of synchronicity then does there perhaps exist a loophole within the quantum theory? Unfortunately not, for when it comes to Schrödinger's equation, which determines the way the wave function changes in time, this too is totally deterministic. It may come as somewhat of a surprise to readers who are non-physicists, but just as with the Newtonian laws of planetary motion, so too the Schrödinger equation is governed by unitary transformations in which the present state of the wave function is totally determined by its state in the past.

Some commentators, however, have speculated that, when it comes to the measurement problem, quantum theory admits a rupture within its causality and allows for the influence of human consciousness. Their argument generally works in the following way: while the changes of a quantum state are totally deterministic, nevertheless as we saw with the case of Schrödinger's Cat, the Schrödinger equation allows for different possibilities or potentialities. However, when it comes to an actual quantum measurement, or observation, only a single, unambiguous outcome is ever recorded. Somehow, a process that seems to lie outside the normal, deterministic laws of physics has condensed all those different possibilities into a single actuality. Does the influence of the human observer, perhaps, play a role in this? Does human consciousness act to collapse the wave function? Could it be that the explanation for parapsychology and even for human consciousness lies in this "collapse of the wave function"?

Some researchers continue to pursue this avenue of enquiry but, to my mind, the issues of quantum measurement, as they are normally discussed, have little to do with the ultimate nature of consciousness. Certainly there is a degree of confusion and a lack of general agreement as to the interpretation of quantum theory among physicists. But what is really called for here is a deeper theory that will unify both quantum theory and relativity and shed light on some of the current difficulties of interpretation. While the measurement problem has generated a host of different interpretations, as far as my own opinions are concerned once the disposition to take a given measurement has been made, using a particular arrangement of experimental apparatus, then the outcome is totally independent of the wishes, desires, memories, dreams and visions of the human observer.

And so, at this level at least, I believe that quantum theory cannot provide us with a convincing explanation for synchronicity and we must therefore look even deeper. Indeed, the whole question of synchronicity causes us to question the very assumptions upon which our science is based; notions of objects that are well-defined in space and time and of the physical interactions between them; assumptions as to the nature of an independent reality, in the sense of spatially localized states whose properties can be defined independent of any observer; assumptions as to the nature of space and of time. It is certainly true that while, at the level of its equations and dynamics, quantum theory may not provide a gap for synchronicity it has certainly called into question many of the assumptions listed above. In particular quantum theory has stressed the holistic nature of the world and in doing so replaces object by process.

But one can go even deeper and question the fragmentation, within our current worldview, between inner and outer, the desire for an objective science, which has no room for values, quali-ties and the nature of subjective experience.

There is an inexhaustible nature to each human being, tree, rock, star and atom. Such inexhaustibility, such *inscape* (to use the term introduced by the poet Gerard Manley Hopkins) sug-gests that there is no most fundamental level, no all-embracing account or law. Each encounter and each perception are fresh attempts to engage the inner authenticity of the world.

Synchronicity transcends the restrictions of time and space. The present is the given of our experience. The present enfolds the past. It is open to creativity so that it can never be totally determined by all that has happened before. All that exists is the present. It is only from within the present that one can discover and unfold the past—as Marcel Proust well understood. And from within the present one can explore those tendencies and patterns that may lead into the future.

The present is an inscape, something that is inexhaustible in its very nature. Within the present are, contained and enfolded, the orders of time. But this is not the mechanical, linear arrow of time of the physicist, rather it is time that we ourselves generate as we seek to unfold the patterns that lie within the present. It is from within this deep well of time, this inexhaustible inscape of the present that the mind excavates the patterns of past and fu-ture, unfolds the dynamics of matter and touches the numinous field of meaning that suffuses the universe.

MEETING THE BLACKFOOT

Chapter 7

Writing, for me, during that early period had mixed motives. On the one hand it was necessary to have an income, in part from consulting and in part from book advances and royalties. But I was also writing to explore ideas and for the fun of writing. During the period after leaving the National Research Council part of the fun came from writing radio plays and from adapting existing works for radio. One of these was taken from Virginia Woolf's *The Waves*. My wife, Maureen, had been reading Woolf's diaries and letters and then going back to the novels. One day I picked up *The Waves*. As I began to read I felt I could hear the voices in my head, as if the whole thing were a radio play. I decided to make the adaptation for radio at two levels of sound. One level, recorded at various locations, referred to the external events in the character's lives—a walk, eating together, and so on. The other level recorded in the studio and heard over the external sounds, was a contrapuntal play of voices as the characters expressed their inner thoughts.

For the stage I wrote *Balancing Acts*, a piece for two characters who meet, fall in love, live together, fall out of love then separate. A rather obvious plot, but again a chance to work in counterpoint for the human voice.

All this was exciting but I also had to produce another book if I were to help pay the rent. Sometimes the idea of a book just appears and other times it seems to elude me. It is the same with the actual writing. When I lie on the bed dozing or half awake, part of a book will appear to me. At one time I used to try to write it down as soon as I woke, as a rapid scrawl of notes. Now I trust the process more. I know that when I sit down at the computer I will more or less reproduce what came to me. Sometimes it is in the form of a few pages that appear in a relatively polished way. Other times it is a flurry of connected ideas and passages that spill out. They form a ground plan with rough connecting links and some fully formed paragraphs. After that it's a matter of filling in the gaps–a sort of paint by numbers. I can sit and type out three or four thousand words at a time in this way. The real business of writing comes later as this initial draft is polished and I seek the correct word or illustrative example. In this way the writing becomes simpler as the passages are honed down.

There are also times when nothing comes. I know I must write a new book but I have no idea what it should be about. This happened to me in the mid 1980s. For days I had been wandering around the house. I sat at the computer but nothing came. I'd pick up a book and leaf through without enthusiasm. I'd go into the garden with good intentions but if I couldn't write, neither could I weed the garden or fix a broken fence. I was in limbo. I was stuck. Suspended. Then one book caught my attention. It contained photographs of Native American faces taken in the nineteenth century. The photographer had used the large plate cameras that gave an incredible definition to the images. They were rich and textured and the faces themselves seemed to speak of an ancient connection to the landscape.

I was looking at these faces when the telephone rang. A man who announced himself as Leroy Little Bear invited me to a meeting on a Blackfoot reservation in Alberta. I was confused and kept insisting that he was speaking to the wrong person. (Some years ago I had had a series of invitations to conferences quite outside my range of interests but addressed to a Dr Peat–my *doppelgänger*.)

Leroy insisted he was correct. Wasn't I the Peat who had worked with David Bohm? The coincidence was staggering because as we spoke about the Blackfoot I was looking at those Native American faces in the book before me.

I agreed to attend but as the day of departure approached I began to feel uneasy. I felt that if I took that flight my life could change. In the end I didn't drive to the airport and decided that this would be another of those conferences I would miss. But I hadn't counted on Leroy who simply rang to say he had booked me on a flight for the following morning and that I was expected.

I realized that I was in the grip of some sort of fate and so I flew to Calgary and was picked up by a Mohawk, Brenda La France—who later became a friend—and driven to the reservation. It was there that I first sat in a tepee with a mixture of Native and non-Native people and participated in the pipe ceremony. My meetings with Leroy and others continued on a fairly regular basis and I also went out to the Blackfoot reserve during the Sun Dance. It seemed important to take things further. I was learning about a different worldview that in many ways was congenial to myself as a physicist. But would other scientists think the same?

Around that time the Fetzer Institute in Kalamazoo had asked me to write some study papers. One afternoon while walking by a lake on the Institute's property with Carol Hegedus and Rob Lehman—who was then CEO—I said how wonderful it would be to see a group of scientists and Native elders sitting there and talking. Rob simply said, "Do it." In this way the first Native American/Western scientist dialogue was born. It was there that David Bohm met people who had been speaking the language about which he had dreamed.

The first Europeans to visit the New World felt they had arrived in Eden with vast virgin forests, abundant game and inhabitants who appeared to live in harmony with the land and who were willing to welcome strangers and teach them about

medicinal plants. Philosophers such as John Locke were interested in the way the inhabitants governed themselves, while the
principles of the Iroquois Confederation of Independent Nations
became the blueprint for the American Constitution. The Spanish and Portuguese who arrived in Central and South America
found many of the edible plants were being cultivated–potatoes,
tomatoes, peppers, maize and so on–that today make up a significant percentage of the world's diet. They encountered a culture that had made detailed astronomical observations, created
accurate calendars that not only gave the phases of the moon but
also of Venus. Yet in one of the greatest crimes against humanity
the libraries were burned and the leaders executed.

Encounters with the white man did not go much better in the
North for a very large percentage of the indigenous population
was wiped out by European diseases for which they possessed no
immunity. (Some have suggested that these diseases preceded the
appearance of the Europeans when animals, released from European ships, carried disease that mutated and infected humans.)
In the United States the doctrine of Manifest Destiny allowed
the settlers to claim land as their own and so the Cherokee were
rounded up and sent on the March of Tears where many died.
In other cases blankets infected with smallpox were distributed
to Native people. On top of all this were the Residential Schools
where children were taken from their families, sometimes by
force, and forbidden to speak their Native languages or carry out
their traditional prayers and ceremonies.

I add this long preface to point out that despite this entire
trauma to a people, this genocide and violation of human rights,
a culture did survive. Admittedly reservations are plagued by al-
coholism and drug addition yet there are always those families,
who preserve the traditional ways. This is what we discussed as
we sat in the talking circle in a tepee or in the conference room
of the Fetzer Institute.

There are many, many nations and language families in North

America. The Blackfoot, Cheyenne, Ojibwaj, Cree, Micmaq, Montagnais, Naskapi, to take one example, extend from the Central Plains to the north of Labrador but do share a common language root—as common, that is, as German is to Spanish, or Hindi to English. Just as (with the exception of Hungarian and Finnish) all European languages come from the Indo-European root, so too the languages spoken by the peoples above have a common Algonkin root. This is the language of people who live predominantly by hunting, as opposed, for example, to the Iroquois family of languages.

The Iroquois are farmers–gatherers who live in villages and meet in the Long House. They plant the three sisters–maize, beans and squash and their language is incredibly rich in kinship terms. But what was the nature of the Algonkin family of languages? It is something that came as a great shock to David Bohm. It is a strongly verb-based language that bears some similarities to what Bohm had hoped to achieve with the Rheomode.

To give an example of the misunderstanding of cultures when it comes to language–some time ago an article in a Canadian magazine argued that Native Americans could not be said to have any science, giving as an example the fact that they called the same bird by different names during different times of the year. The writer assumed that because the bird's plumage had changed the ignorant and unobservant Natives believed that there were two different birds with different names. Yet to a Native person, just as a man's name would change depending on his deeds, so too the name of a bird should change as it entered a different phase of its life cycle.

The Blackfoot live in a world of flux. Everything changes, nothing can be fixed. Even a person's name changes during his or her lifetime and, jokingly, they told me that someone with a single personality would seem very boring. Within that flux is a cyclic time–the seasons and the ceremonies come around year after year, just as the sun rises each morning. A society can make a mark in that flux, but that mark will soon pass away unless it is renewed, which is the purpose of the ceremonies. In ancient times the ancestors came into relationship with the powers, energies and spirits of nature, and with the keepers of the animals. These relationships must be honored through a variety of ceremonies.

Each morning, for example, someone will face the rising sun with a lit peace pipe. But no one would be so naïve as to believe the ceremony *causes* the sun to rise. Rather it is a renewal of that harmony between order on earth and that in the cosmos. Likewise, the Sun Dance is carried out each year for the harmony of the entire cosmos and its relationship to the people.

By carrying out a ceremony each person is engaged in an act of renewal. All of nature is alive and the Blackfoot are in relationship to it. In the sweat lodge they may commune with the keeper of the Bear and never refer to this most sacred of animals directly. They are in relationship with the trees, which are alive, and certain stones that are alive, to the beings in the air, and those in the earth.

All this is expressed in their language. For, if you want to know their science, you must learn their language. Take as an example the phrase in Montagnais *Hipiskapigoka iagusit*. In 1729 a Jesuit priest composed a dictionary and translated this as "the sorcerer sings the sick man" which illustrates a great deal about a clash of cultures. To begin with, take note of the word "sorcerer." It reflects the notion, current at that time, that anything to do with traditional ways had to be the work of the Devil. But there is a subtler undercurrent. In our Western worldview a doctor cures a person. There is a sick person and an agent of change–the doctor–who does something to this sick person. This is the world of the subject-object-verb languages. On the other hand the Algonkin languages are all strongly verb-based. It would be closer to say that "singing is going on" and out of this primary process is revealed a medicine person and a sick man. Indeed songs themselves are beings. It is not so much that we remember and sing them but that the song sings itself.

The language and the worldview, that all is flux, enfold each other. Likewise such a language does not lend itself so easily to the creation of categories. "What is in that drawer," we ask? "Knives," is the reply. But to a Native person there will only be individual knives, each made by someone for a particular use. We have a general category of fish that includes salmon, goldfish and sharks. For the Micmaq there are "processes in water."

One consequence of such languages is that the speakers do not divide up the world into categories of binary oppositions. In our world things are either good or bad, people are for us or against us, agreements must be in black and white. The world of the Blackfoot, however, is one of constant flux and rather than weeding out the good from the bad they are more concerned with harmony and balance.

DIALOGUE

Excursion VII

D avid Bohm had spent much of his life speaking of transformation and "undivided wholeness." Wholeness was
essential to the quantum theory for, at the moment of measurement, the observer and observed form an unanalyzable whole.
This was also an essential factor in Bohm's many conversations
with Jiddu Krishnamurti who, speaking of the mind, would say
that "the thinker is thought, the observer is the observed."

The other element in his thought was transformation. As a
student under Oppenheimer, Bohm had studied Karl Marx and
believed that social transformation was possible. Within a ratio-
nally ordered Marxist state, he believed at the time, it would be
possible for human beings to transform themselves and behave in
rational ways. Indeed, his first significant contribution to physics–the theory of plasmas in metals–was inspired by his belief
that there could be individual freedom within the collective. In
Bohm's plasma theory each individual electron contributes to the
collective oscillations of the plasma. In turn these electrons become relatively free because of the plasma's shielding effect.

Later, disillusioned with the Soviet experiment, Bohm turned
to Krishnamurti and believed that it was possible for the human
mind to become silent and in that silence to transform–even in
the literal sense of involving permanent physical changes in the
neurons. If the minds of only ten people could experience such a

transformation, Bohm once told me, then the effect would reach out progressively to the whole of society.

But as time went on Bohm began to notice that those around Krishnamurti were related to the teacher like spokes on a wheel are to its center, but it was a wheel that had no circumference–there was no link between them, only between each individual and Krishnamurti. Bohm came to feel that each person has a personal, a cosmic and a social dimension. In Krishnamurti's case the social dimension was not being addressed. But how was this social dimension to be engaged?

During a period of depression Bohm had sought psychiatric help from Patrick de Maré who had been experimenting with therapy groups. In addition to groups designed for patient therapy de Maré had also created another group for people who were not in therapy. The idea of this latter group was to explore the notion of what could perhaps be called a form of social therapy–not directed to individual neuroses and the like but to the general dysfunction of society as a whole.

Bohm, along with his friend, the Nobel Prize winner Maurice Wilkins, became part of the social therapy group. In this way Bohm began to see that a form of dialogue could be the key to social transformation. Now he began to experiment on his own by setting up dialogue groups of some thirty to forty people who would meet every week. Each of us, Bohm argued, has a set of fixed non-negotiable positions. To take one example, we may be firm believers in a woman's right to have control over her own body or we may believe that from the moment of conception an embryo is a living being with an immortal soul. If the topic of abortion should come up between two such people it would either lead to argument and a breakdown in communication or they would simply avoid ever bringing up such a topic when together. In either case the individuals would be left with their fixed positions and with a restricted communication.

However in a large group there will always be others who do

not hold strongly to either position. Such people can moderate between two extreme positions and support the tension that exists in the room. In this way it becomes possible for a person to remain with an inner sense of anger, for example, but without fracturing all communication. Thanks to the moderating or slowing down effect of the group, a person may now be able to stay with their strong feelings and not immediately react with some harsh attack or defensive position. The aim of the dialogue process is not so much to resolve a fixed position but for members of the group to begin to understand how such positions are structured and how they act to produce tensions within the body and mind. The key is not so much to modify a particular position but to understand how it comes about and how it continues to operate within the body, often producing strong reaction which is not always clearly understood by the person involved.

Through dialogue, Bohm believed, people gain a greater inner awareness. At the same time this movement in and out of fixed non-negotiable positions has a wider social effect. Bohm believed that language has a deep effect on how we perceive the world and the ways in which we act. Yet language is a social construct containing many subtle enfolded assumptions about the world. There is a famous remark of Confucius who was asked by the rulers of China what action they should take at a particular time of crisis. "First purify the language," the sage replied.

There is a story I once heard about a woman studying for her PhD who asked how it was possible for ordinary human beings to contemplate nuclear destruction on a large scale. To this end she obtained a job in the Pentagon where she could observe generals playing war games. After several months her supervisor noticed a subtle change in the way she was writing up her results and felt that her objectivity had been compromised. It was only after some serious soul searching that the woman realized that the idea of death and destruction had been distanced from her by the particular use of language employed by Pentagon staff where words like death and victims were never used, but rather people spoke of "collateral damage," "preemptive strikes" and so on. A similar distancing effect had also been used in Nazi Germany where Jews, transported in trucks heading for the gas chambers, were referred to as "merchandise."

Bohm's own view was that by exploring the use of language within a dialogue group it would be possible to effect subtle but important changes that would then trickle out into society as a whole.

Since Bohm's early experiments the notion of "dialogue" seems to have caught on with a number of groups. For example, in 1994 MIT began the "Dialogue Project" under William Isaacs. But of course dialogue is not new, indeed it is probably one of the oldest of social constructs—a group who sit around a fire at night and talk. In this context I had the privilege of attending a circle on the Blackfoot reservation in Alberta. We met at night in a tepee and talk went around a circle. In this particular case each person spoke in turn. One might reflect on an experience in the past and so on until it came to a woman who spoke of her battle with alcohol and her guilt at the way she had treated her children. Now in any comfortable middle class environment the immediate reaction would be for people to touch this woman, to say "thank you for sharing," "we feel your pain" and so on and so forth. But there was none of this in the tepee for the next person sang a song and the one after this told a joke. At first I didn't understand what was happening until I realized that this was an entire movement within the circle. It was not a case of individuals "spilling their guts" as with an encounter group but of thoughts and feelings that were the expression of the group as a whole.

In our everyday world a feeling or a memory may arise and we tend to hold on to it, to soak ourselves in pity, or anger or grief. But what I experienced was feelings that arose and died down again—they were not clung to. It was as if the circle itself was the primary reality and the people within the circle were secondary—expressions of the movement within the entire circle.

To a lesser extent I have noticed something similar in the small Italian village where I now live—and much more about that later. In the summer people sit in a circle in the piazza and talk together during the evening. When it comes time to make a decision or take some action it seems that people simply know what to do—not so much via a formal decision-making process but an overall flow of meaning that is shared by everyone.

So where does this leave dialogue? For me the jury is out at the moment. I think it is going to be very easy to turn the whole thing from an interesting experiment into yet another technique that can be practiced by business people or taught in leadership courses. And armed with a diploma in "dialogue" anyone can become a consultant! Yet, whatever happens, in many parts of the world people will sit around a fire at night and talk and sing and maybe in a subtle way an effect will ripple out to bring about change.

DAVID BOHM AND THE IMPLICATE ORDER

Chapter 8

B eing outside the confines of the NRC also allowed me to continue to work with David Bohm. Each year we would meet for several weeks at Bohm's home in Edgware, north London. Generally we would begin with a long walk, since Bohm talked best while he was walking. We would then return for lunch and I would write up notes on our conversation while Bohm rested. For the rest of the afternoon we would go over my notes and amplify our discussions. Then it was time for dinner and the underground back to the center of London. It was in this way we wrote the book *Science, Order and Creativity* together.

Bohm's long-time associate, Basil Hiley, described Bohm's thinking as a spiral. For a time he would focus on one idea. It may be something in philosophy, or a problem in physics. Then he would appear to lose interest and abandon it totally and move on to some other problem. Yet months or even years later he would return and approach the same subject in a new way.

One thread in Bohm's thinking had been the problem of reconciling quantum theory and relativity. In one sense the two theories needed each other's support, yet despite attempts to make a marriage, the two theories remained incompatible. Physicists felt they had to come up with new ideas or that some new mathematical approach was needed. For Bohm that wasn't sufficient. What was required, he thought, was a radically new order in physics.

Only from this new order, this new way of looking, would a new and deeper theory emerge.

Classical physics describes a world of independent objects, each possessing objective properties. These exist in well-defined positions in space and interact with each other via forces and fields. Bohm called this the *explicate order*. But this explicate order was at odds with quantum theory which is all about wholeness. What was needed was a radically new order at this level.

Throughout the 1960s, Bohm had a long exchange of letters with the artist Charles Biederman. Their discussions ranged over many topics including perception and the way art could transform the mind. In particular, they began to discuss the nature of order, with Biederman drawing on examples of order within the paintings of Monet and Cézanne. In such paintings each part is intimately related to the whole. There is an anecdote about the art dealer Vollard who had given an enormous number of sittings to Cézanne. Finally the painter left two very tiny areas on one hand blank. He told Vollard that if he were to fill them in he would then have to repaint the entire canvas. Bohm, for his part, argued that if he could discover a mathematics that would describe the order of such paintings it would be exactly the mathematics needed for the quantum theory.

Eventually Bohm proposed a new order he called the *implicate order*. This, he felt, would be more appropriate to describe the quantum theory. It is a sort of enfolded order in which each part can be found within the whole and the whole in each part. Bohm would sometimes give the example of a hologram. If you tear off a piece of a photograph you will see only part of, for example, a face. But if you take a part of a hologram you will continue to see the whole face as each part is enfolded across the entire hologram.

Reality, Bohm felt, is close to the implicate order. Aspects of the implicate order unfold into the explicit forms we see around us–the explicate order–and then fold back again. The mind itself is structured in the same way. Much of it operates at the implicate level with occasional explicate forms being thrown up. All our discussions on these topics found their way into *Science, Order and Creativity*.

Having completed the book, and thanks to the generosity of Jack Himmelstein–co-founder of the Center for Mediation in Law–Bohm and I continued to meet, this time at the Bailey Farms, near Ossining, New York. Our conversations were very general and ranged from physics to the future of society, from philosophy to the nature of thought and perception. We also began to discuss the meaning of the implicate order. What sort of structuring principles did it have? Was there a relationship between these principles and Jung's archetypes–the dynamical structuring principles of the collective unconscious? Did the implicate order exist as a sort of object, process or fundamental level, or should it be thought of more as a descriptive device? And what sort of mathematics would describe this implicate order?

I was also concerned with what I felt to be a somewhat static element in the implicate order. The explicate emerged from the implicate and could be enfolded back again. The explicate was dynamical and full of change. But how did change occur in the implicate and did the explicate bring anything back into the implicate? Where was the new and the creative in all this? In some ways the idea appeared almost Platonic. Although at the time I could not formulate my objections as clearly and forcefully as I would have wished I still felt uneasy about the one-way aspect of his approach.

I had not realized that Rupert Sheldrake had been making similar objections. Nor that Bohm and Hiley were working on a related notion in physics, the superquantum potential. At all events, as we continued to talk Bohm's position began to change and he now included a *super-implicate order* that could carry back information from the explicate order and bring about change in the implicate. In this way creativity and novelty were introduced into the overall scheme.

Independent of our meetings and discussions I had also been thinking about what I called the *space between*. It was an idea that could be applied in many areas, particularly to describe what happens when you look at art or read a work of literature. It is the space that lies between the observer and the observed; it is the space of the creative act that brings a poem or a painting to life. Therefore when, on one of the next occasions that we met, Bohm mentioned an *order between* it was clear that we had been thinking along parallel lines. This notion of something that lies between seemed an ideal subject for our next book.

In Bohm's case he had arrived at this idea while thinking about terms of what he called "fixed non-negotiable positions." Throughout his life he had been concerned about the transformation of society and the role of the collective and the individual in such a process. Now he began to focus on the origin of conflict. Not with the intention of resolving some particular social or political issue, but more of seeing the whole psychological nature of the way conflict arises. Fixed non-negotiable positions involve those moments in a relationship where one of the parties has reached a sticking point where they are unable to move from a strongly held moral or philosophical conviction. At such a juncture the discussion will either degenerate into angry argument or into that icy coldness that indicates that a relationship has come to an end.

This had always been a concern of Bohm's. After all his own ideas had been met with rejection from the fixed positions of orthodox physics. He also related the story of how in their early days Bohr and Einstein had been so close that they felt love for each other. Yet towards the end of their lives the two men had nothing to say to each other. This breakdown in communication, Bohm argued, was brought about by the particular ways each man used language. They appeared to be dialoguing but each was using language in such a subtly different way–the language about the physics they were doing. There was no longer a *space between* these two men–they had ceased to communicate. In many ways the absence of an *order between* also lay at the heart of the failure to marry quantum theory (Bohr) and relativity (Einstein).

The issue therefore became that of discovering ways of moving beyond fixed non-negotiable positions and arriving at an order between. At that time the approach known as conflict resolution had become very fashionable. Bohm tended to be critical of its underlying philosophy and felt that it was too easy to move into a position of compromise where each party makes a series of small concessions in order to reach agreement. For this reason we were focusing on the order beyond or rather the *order between and beyond*. For my part the general idea we were pursuing would, I hoped, illuminate that highly creative movement which occurs when one first finds oneself moving between two positions–opposing ideas, binary oppositions, the poem and the imagination, the work of art and one's inner life, Cézanne and the landscape. It is in this movement that something new is born, some space is opened, that was never anticipated in either of those two positions alone.

I had also been reading about poststructuralism and deconstruction and while I found the style of writing unnecessarily obscure there did seem to be areas that could be brought into our general discussion. We continued to meet each day and develop the ideas. But Bohm's health was now failing. Some years before he had had a heart bypass operation and increasingly his heart seemed weakened. While we continued to meet and talk I became concerned that our book would never be completed. Indeed, Bohm died before we began serious work on the chapters.

Our last encounter was at the Fetzer Institute on the occasion of the first Native American Elders/Western Scientists circle, referred to in the previous chapter. The elders realizing that Bohm was unwell said that during one ceremony an object would be passed around the circle–I think it may have been an eagle feather. They asked us each to donate some of our energy that would then be available to him when the object reached him. In fact Bohm's energies revived and at the end of the weekend he actually danced to the drum—an event I could never have imagined would ever take place.

Following the meeting we both stayed on in Kalamazoo to talk. Bohm kept returning to the philosophy of Hegel. As a student at Berkley he had read Marx and was told that "Marx put Hegel on his feet." Later Bohm discovered Hegel for himself and felt that Marxism had distorted Hegel. As he put it, "Marx had stood Hegel on his head!!" From that time on Hegel was the key philosopher for Bohm.

Shortly after our last discussion Bohm went to Prague where he became unwell. His heart was severely strained and his health much worse. One day, on his return to London, he telephoned his wife from his office at Birkbeck College where he was working with Basil Hiley. He told her that he was on his way home and added, "You know, it's tantalizing. I feel I'm on the edge of something." When the taxi reached his front door Bohm was dead.

ACTIVE INFORMATION AND QUANTUM MIND

Excursion VIII

Physics of the eighteenth century dealt with the movement and transformation of matter. The nineteenth century introduced the notion that various forms of energy–work, heat, electrical, chemical, biological, etc–are mutually interconvertable, transforming one into the other according to the laws of thermodynamics. Then, at the start of the twentieth century, Einstein's formula $E=mc^2$ showed that the mutual transformation of matter and energy was possible. And now, in the twenty-first century, we should perhaps entertain the notion of a triad (matter, energy, information) in place of the duality matter-energy.

It is certainly true that, with the rise of the computer, digital representations of all kinds and electronic communications, the twentieth century became the age of information. Yet information is generally treated as something passive, e.g. in the Information Theory of Shannon and Weaver information is treated as cargo being shipped from sender to receiver. If the transmission line is noisy then some of that information will be lost and so engineers are concerned with improving the "signal to noise ratio." But information, as considered in this essay, is something very different from a passive signal sent between two agents.

Information has always played an active role in our lives. Vision is a case in point. As signals move from the retina along the optic nerve they meet a flood of information coming down from the visual cortex in the brain. This downward flow arises out of the various strategies employed in seeing and has the effect of actively screening, coding and comparing incoming signals. In this sense our vision is not a passive gathering of information as with a television camera, but prehensile or reaching outward to grasp the world. We begin to see something and create a hypothesis of what that could be. Now muscles around the eye are directed to scan the scene and gather additional clues. Incoming clues are interrogated by information-checking systems that flow downward from the visual cortex. In this way evidence for a hypothesis is built up, or the entire hypothesis is denied–that dark shape is not a tiger but the shadow made by a tree. Vision is very far from some passive activity, rather it is purposeful, an activity of information that extends throughout the entire visual system from the muscles around the eyes to the cortex itself.

The immune system could also be considered as an activity of information. It constantly scans the environment looking for harmful intrusions into the body. As an active pattern-recognition system it is perhaps as complex as the brain itself.

The analogy can also be made with language, since the word, as information, also acts within the body. This corporaliziation of words was recognized by Wilhelm Reich and later by Jacques Lacan. In this sense the word is made flesh and dwells within us. Language is not a passive carrier of information but an activity in its own right. Language exerts an influence on how we think, act and perceive. In turn, social changes are reflected in transformations of language. It is the job of the poet to transform society by purifying language and transforming the activity of words. Indeed, as we learned in the section on dialogue and language, it becomes the task of each of us to take responsibility for language and help it retain its power and purity.

Maybe the activity of information extends right into the quantum domain. David Bohm's ontological, or causal, version of the quantum theory interpretation invokes active information in a particularly interesting way.

In conventional physics the various pushes and pulls of the world–gravity, magnetism, electrical fields and so on–can be represented by potentials. The bigger the potential, the more a push or pull is experienced. To this conventional approach Bohm added something new called the *quantum potential*. He wrote down an equation to express the way an electron, or any other quantum particle, moves. This equation contained the ordinary potentials of physics plus the new term–the quantum potential. Bohm was able to show that if the quantum potential was put as zero then his equation would represent the classical world. But in the cases where the quantum potential is not zero all the curious effects of the quantum world are present. (Bohm could also show that applying a mathematical transformation to his equation would produce conventional quantum theory. In his approach, however, what perhaps could be called the *quantum strangeness* was all collected in one term–the quantum potential.)

What was new and strange about the quantum potential was that, unlike other potentials, its effect did not depend on the strength of the potential but on its *form*: i.e. the potential's effect on an electron depended on the complexity of its overall pattern. What does this mean? Bohm was able to show that this quantum potential contains information about the conditions that surround an electron. Hence his use of the term information, i.e. *in-form-ation*. During an experiment this information is *active*, i.e. it can act on the electron to influence the path it takes. But once the experiment is over and the electron has, for example, been registered by a Geiger counter the information is *inactive*.

To illustrate the theory, Bohm used to give the example of a ship that approaches a harbor in deep fog. The ship is driven by a powerful engine but the captain does not know the right direction in which to navigate. This is given by a radar signal, a very weak signal that, however, is rich in information about the location of the harbor. In this way a very weak energy but rich in information, directs a large energy, that of the ship's engine.

In other words Bohm is now suggesting that information has an activity of its own. In particular it in-forms, or gives form to, energy. And just as matter and energy are mutually convertible, the same may be true of matter-energy and information. Thus we must remain open to the possibility that a new form of triad exists in the world

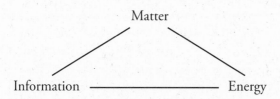

A television set is powered by energy that arrives from the plug in the wall. But this gross energy is augmented by very subtle energy–the signal beamed from the television transmitting station that is rich in information about pictures and sounds. In this way the circuits in the television set "read" the information in the signal and convert them into speech and moving images. Bohm used to joke that because the electron is also able to "read" the information in the quantum potential it must be at least as complicated as a television set!

But this was not really a joke, for Bohm asserted that the electron possesses a *proto-mind* and that mind has always been present from the beginning of the universe. In fact mind and matter have always been inseparable.

If the idea of an electron as a tiny ball guided by a quantum potential does not appear all that attractive then one must remember that this was only the first version. In the next version of the theory the electron is no longer a particle but a process, a process that is constantly unfolding out of and enfolding into the entire universe. In turn this process is determined by a *super-quantum potential*.

MEETINGS WITH ARTISTS

Chapter 9

Following Bohm's death, friends had asked me if I would write something about him but I declined. Then I began to hear rumors that a popular science writer was going to begin a biography of Bohm. I was not convinced that such a person would be capable of doing a good job so after discussing the idea with Bohm's widow, Saral, I decided that I would write the book and found an excellent editor in Jeff Robbins at Addison-Wesley.

I had already accumulated a great deal of material on Bohm. We had exchanged letters and on many occasions I had made notes of our conversations together. Now I had to track down his relations and friends in the United States. I also began to see the patterns of Bohm's life as a greater whole.

As we have seen, Bohm had spent much of his life speaking of transformation and of "undivided wholeness." Wholeness was also essential to the quantum theory for, at the moment of a measurement, the observer and observed form an unanalyzable whole.

Wholeness and transformation, these were the cornerstones of Bohm's thinking. They opened doors for people who read, spoke or studied with Bohm, yet ironically they did not always function in his own life. In his many encounters Bohm yearned for a radical transformation of consciousness that always eluded him. He wrote about wholeness yet, as his friend the psychiatrist,

David Shainberg, pointed out, it was not always present in his personal life. Only history will judge the significance of Bohm's contributions. If these are of importance then he may well be one of those "wounded healers" whose very wounds enable them to cure others.

At all events fragmentation as well as wholeness seemed to be a pattern in Bohm's life and work, for the more I researched his life the more it appeared to have been lived in a number of separate compartments. In meeting friends and relatives I would constantly come across some unexpected anecdote or angle on his life. For example, some of those who had known him well during the 1950s were not aware that he had been a Marxist and even, for a time, joined the Communist party. In later life he did not always reveal to others the importance of his relationship to Krishnamurti. In my own case I once discussed J.G. Bennet, one of Ouspensky's followers, with him but Bohm never revealed that the two men had had many conversations together.

Personal reminiscences are the spice of life but a biography has to be backed up with documentation and so I needed to track down Bohm's letters. Never having written a biography before I was surprised to learn how personally attached a recipient can be to letters written decades before. I knew that while the copyright of the content of a letter remains with the writer, or their estate, the person who receives such letters owns the physical piece of paper. All I wanted to do was to make photocopies, or at best take notes, from Bohm's letters but in some cases this proved difficult to achieve.

One situation involved an ex-girlfriend of Bohm's from his early years who had a remarkable collection of letters and documents. These were not only from Bohm himself but included letters, documents and even hand-written manuscripts of some of the leading writers, artists and thinkers who had gathered in Princeton during the thirties and forties—many of whom had fled from Germany to escape the Nazis. These extremely valuable documents were not stored systematically. Instead they were left in piles around her apartment, under furniture and even spread over her stove, kitchen counters and the bed in which she slept.

When she told me of Bohm's letters and manuscripts I simply had to have them photocopied. I tried in vain to gain permission. She was happy to talk to me, but would not let me see what Bohm had written during the 1950s, one of the most significant periods in his life both scientifically and politically. It was clear that this woman had become eccentric in her old age.

Finally I had an intuition and this time visited with my wife, Maureen, and then left the two of them alone together. Finally the ex-girlfriend agreed and began to stuff letters and manuscripts into several plastic bags. Next she wandered around her apartment picking up old clothing and also stuffing these into bags. As they walked down the road to the photocopy shop passersby were stopped and offered gifts of old clothes.

Maureen began to photocopy the letters. She got through quite a few until she heard, "No, that's enough" and the plastic bags were taken from her. The material proved invaluable for it gave first-hand evidence of Bohm's life in exile in Brazil. It also included a theory of the cosmos of mind and matter that Bohm had created while still in high school.

In addition to my research in New York I also had to travel to California to meet with relations and with Bohm's old school friend, Mort Weiss. Finally I would need to go to London. Not only did his widow, Saral, his long-term associate, Basil Hiley, and his many friends live in London but also there would be other documents to read.

But before I relate yet another pathway that opened for me because of that trip I'd like to make an aside to mention the creative nature that some organizations can exhibit. I have heard so many stories of the way people struggle to obtain funding from large agencies, of the time they have to set aside to write a grant proposal, of the rigidity they encounter, of the frustrations they experience. But this time I'd like to stress the positive. One experience had been the Fetzer Institute's spontaneous response to my chance remarks that it would be interesting to have a group of scientists and Native American elders sit in a circle.

Here is another example. On one of my trips to New York before leaving for London I had lunch with Charles Halpern who was at that time CEO of the Nathan Cummings Foundation. He mentioned that the Foundation funded in several areas, one of which was art and another the environment, but the two had never been put together. Why not, while I was in London, hunt around and see how the fields overlapped? This I did and discovered that quite a few artists were involved in environmental projects–repairing dry stone sheep folds, reviving older varieties of apple trees and so on. This was also the time when people were protesting against the building of motorways that would pass through woodlands and other environmental areas considered valuable. Many of these protesters were artists who lived in trees or in underground burrows.

After being in London for some time I wrote a report for Halpern. In turn, he suggested mounting an exhibition in New York, or running a conference. I explained to him that the particular artists involved would not be sympathetic to either suggestion but that they would love a good dinner. And so the Foundation paid for an excellent dinner held at a Russian restaurant in London–some of the artists arriving from long distances by bicycle. The lively discussion was recorded and transcribed as a further report. One suggestion was to mount an environmental opera in New York–a proposal that is still on the table.

But to return to the main story. I realized I would have to be in London for several months and so we planned to rent out our house in Ottawa and reserved an apartment in London starting in December 1994. We handed everything over to an agent who, several days later rang to say that while he had not yet rented the house he had received a very attractive offer to buy. There was only one problem—we had to be out of the house on the first of August.

We only had six weeks to move out and store all our belongings. It was at this point that Maureen said, "Let's go to Italy." She loved the Sienese school of painting and so we spoke to an Italian travel agent in Ottawa who promised to arrange an apartment for us in Siena. By July 31st all our belongings would be in storage. We would spend the night in a motel and the next afternoon fly directly to Rome. There was only one problem; the travel agent had not yet given us the address of our apartment in Siena. In fact, as the date of departure drew closer she had become increasingly evasive as to its location. She claimed that she didn't even know the phone number to pass on to our family and friends. At all events she told us to relax and that she would call us later.

On the morning of the flight we went to her office where she finally admitted that there was no apartment. The best she could do was to give us a bedroom in someone's house quite close to the center of the city—in fact when we did arrive by taxi it turned out to be several kilometers away. Instead of living in a medieval city we were now trapped in a small room in a modern housing complex from which we could see the towers of Siena in the distance. We simply had to find an alternative and over the next few days we visited every estate agency listed. But August was the month of the Palio (the famous horse race that takes place in the piazza in the center of the city). In addition, Siena was full of foreign students attending its many Italian language schools. At each encounter we were told the same story: there was nothing available.

I had heard of apartments in Portugal that were not too expensive; maybe we should forget about Italy and move on. It was while we were discussing this possibility that Maureen spotted what looked like another agency, but one that was not on the list we had been given. As we approached the door we saw a group of people standing in a circle, speaking in German, and looking down at the ground. We stopped to see what had caught their attention. It was a golden scarab beetle. At that moment I recalled Jung's story of the remarkable synchronicity in which the scarab from a patient's dream flew through his window. "They'll have an apartment for us!" I said. We went in and heard the same story, "Nothing available." But, as we were leaving, the secretary told us she had a friend with a house to sell in a small village, maybe it would be possible to rent it on a temporary basis. A few days later we were driven some thirty-five kilometers south of Siena to a remote medieval hilltop village surrounded by thickly wooded hills. We had arrived at Pari where we were to spend the next three and a half months.

How many visitors to Italy stay in the big cities and make the Grand Tour? How few have the opportunity to stay amongst people who see few strangers, speak no English and live as their ancestors have lived for hundreds of years?

I have often been asked about what I did for the first months I spent in Pari. My answer has always been, "Nothing."

"Oh yes," would come the reply. "I understand all that but what did you actually *do*? Did you read a lot? Did you make notes for your next book? I suppose you wrote a lot of letters."

"No," I always responded, "I did nothing."

"Then you must have been thinking a great deal."

The truth is that we arrived with a couple of suitcases and no books. We were in a house without a telephone. We didn't have a car and there were only two buses in and out of the village each day. I did bring a laptop but hardly switched it on. Instead, each day I would sit in a deckchair and look out over the landscape. My mind was more or less a blank. I really did nothing. I thought of nothing. There were times when I became quite uneasy and thought, "I really must begin to plan another book. I must investigate some new ideas." But that feeling would soon pass. Instead we took walks in the valley. You can't force the creative act. It simply appears when it is ready. Those who are practically-minded may say that I wasted my time. On the other hand material was gathering in my subconscious mind for a new series of books.

The people of the village told me that Italy is the most beautiful country in the world, that Tuscany is the most beautiful region of Italy and that Pari is the most beautiful village in Tuscany. From time to time I would meet Aladino, an old man driving his tractor home from working in the fields. Aladino would take me by the arm and point to the land. "Look," he would say. I'd look and nod and say something like "Beautiful." "No," he'd say, "Look…look!" as if to force me to see the land through his eyes.

Of course when I say that I did nothing while in Pari that is not strictly true. Something was happening deep down inside me for, months later, I had a surge of creative activity that expressed itself in a number of new books and ideas.

Finally Pari had to come to an end and in the weeks preceding our flight to London I had disturbing dreams of traffic and crowded streets. The peace of Pari was overwhelming and part of me did not want to lose what we had discovered by pure chance. But things cannot last and so we found ourselves in London. Very quickly I adjusted to life in one of my favorite cities in the world. London may be big but you always have the feeling that you are living in a neighborhood. Our first stop of several months was an apartment close to Russell Square. Our second to Blackheath where we could enjoy a Sunday afternoon stroll in Greenwich Park.

Our original intention had been to return to Canada as soon as my research for the Bohm biography was complete. We would find a new house and settle back again. But after several months in London I felt that I was there to stay. And so we flew back to Canada and arranged to have our belongings shipped from storage to London. This included the painful experience of going through our library of ten thousand books and giving away hundreds—we just couldn't afford to ship all of them.

London opened up a new door for me. I had always been interested in art and in the way artists look at the world. Not only artists who work in traditional ways, with paint, stone or photography but also those who work with ideas and concepts. Much of my time was now spent talking to artists. These included Anish Kapoor, Antony Gormley, Janine Antoni (who was in London from New York) Bruce Gilchrist, Siraj Izhar, Susan Derges, Cornelia Parker and Rachel Whiteread. I made visits to the studios of Gormley and Kapoor and had many long conversations with them. When Kapoor had a retrospective at the Hayward Gallery I gave one of the guided walks around the exhibition. Bronac Ferran from the Arts Council of England was present and asked me what I would do if she gave me some money. I told her I would find a nice comfortable room, some good restaurants and gather a group of artists and scientists together to talk.

Yet again an organization responded in a creative way and a few months later we all met at the October Gallery in London. I have always believed that highly creative things can occur when you allow structures to develop spontaneously, rather than having a plan of talks and breakaway groups. And so we simply sat and talked together. My only intervention was to invite two contact dancers to move our debates onto a physical plane when they became over-intellectual.

During our discussions the physicist Basil Hiley explained his notions of pre-space–a mathematical structure existing before space-time and matter–to the sculptor Gormley. This led Gormley to make a radical change in his work with the piece *Quantum Cloud* that is now mounted over the river Thames. Another participant demonstrated apparatus that displayed fluctuations in heartbeat. The artist Ansuman Biswas hooked himself up and went into a meditative state. This gave him the idea for a performance piece in which he would display his body state during meditation. This later took place at Headlands in San Francisco.

This interest in art also enabled me to become a peripatetic "scientist in residence," spending time at art schools in London, Oxford, Bristol and Brighton. The residences were short but stimulating. Generally they would start with a lecture, then over the following days students would approach me and we would discuss their work, or they would ask me to explain the more technical details about some aspect of science.

That year in London also marked the ninetieth birthday of the composer Sir Michael Tippett. Tippett's music was being performed all over London. I went to several concerts after which Tippett would spring onto the platform, still looking youthful and accept applause. Tippett was someone I wanted to meet; after all he had been influenced by his encounter with Jungian ideas. After writing to him I was granted a half-hour interview but when Tippett called for a bottle of wine to be opened I realized I'd be there all afternoon. Another composer I talked to was Jonathan Harvey who was working with the inscape of electronic sound. My other contacts were with Jungians. I had many conversations with Christopher Hauke, who went on to write *Jung and the Postmodern: The Interpretation of Realities* as well as editing *Jung and Film*.

In my discussions with Kapoor we had asked, "Where is the art? Is it in the stone? The mind of the artist? The mind of the viewer? Or in some space between?" This struck a chord with the Jungians who asked, "Where is the healing?" We therefore planned a meeting of artists and Jungians to discuss the idea of this "order between"–a notion I had also explored with Bohm. Unfortunately I was only able to attend the first of these because, as things turned out, I was not destined to stay in London for much longer.

ART AND INSCAPE

Excursion IX

The word inscape is taken from the works of the English poet Gerard Manley Hopkins who wrote of "the inner deep down dwelling of things." To see the world as inscape is to contrast it with the world as landscape in which passive observers regard nature from an elevated, protected and remote viewpoint. As landscape, nature becomes a collection of objects and interactions, the product of inexorable laws operating upon fundamental elements of reality. But to see the world as inscape is to take each experience and each perception as unique and authentic. It is to realize that each person, rock and tree has infinite possibility and unbounded richness. To see the world as inscape, in which each element and each experience stands uniquely upon its own authenticity, offers a profound challenge to the way we think and theorize about the world. Indeed, we must now seek a new logic of perception and a new manner of integrating our observations and experiences into a coherent whole.

But this is no mere exercise in abstraction, for all our experience has the potential to participate within inscape. Our authentic relationships with those whom we love and for whom we feel deep compassion can never be reduced to plans, programs, acts of control or objective observations. Rather, our engagement with each person, rock and tree or, for that matter, atom is inexhaustible in its inner nature, boundlessly subtle and irreducible to any single level or set of rules.

Once we are willing to accept each experience of nature as unique and inexhaustible in its richness then we have opened the door to a radically different vision of perception. For we too are inscape, each one of us is an inexhaustible, essential mystery and center of sacredness. To speak of perception is to speak of the merging of horizons, the fusing of the inscape of nature with our own inner richness; it is to enter into something mysterious and direct, an endlessly subtle movement between inner and outer.

Of course it is always possible for thought to analyze and theorize about the world. The history of science shows how enormously powerful has been this combination of analysis and observation. But I want to suggest that we must now acknowledge the essential limitations of this process. Every analysis is incomplete and provisional; every experiment is dependent upon a wider context; any set of laws is conditional; any attempt to reduce nature to a most fundamental level is ultimately subverted by the very act of reduction itself.

Provided that we consider nature only as landscape, then thought is still able to analyze the world and engage in a play of forms; a dance in which thoughts become the objects of the world. When each object is external to us and, it is assumed, known in its entirety then integrating the world simply becomes a matter of fitting all those independent pieces of experience together and discovering how they interact. When nature is landscape, each object can be reduced to some more fundamental level in which the elements of reality follow the basic and inexorable laws of physics. Integration, within such a world of landscape, becomes simply a matter of extending the technical limits of human thought—by no means simple yet a goal that is achievable in principle.

Seeing the world as landscape goes hand-in-hand with the sort of analytical thinking that takes consistency and logical connectivity as being pre-eminent. Such thinking seeks to fit each new fact or observation into a pre-existing scheme. In that approach, what is new to us is always conditioned so that we find ourselves asking not so much "What is this new thing?" but "How does it fit into what we already know?" Of course the great danger in all this is that each new experience must be stretched and transformed until it takes the form demanded of it by the mind's schema. When logic stands firm and each new experience is required to pass the test of consistency then the world begins to lose its immediacy and vibrancy.

Yet, once we admit the inscape of the world into our lives the carpet of logical consistency is pulled out from under our feet and we discover that we are no longer standing upon its firm foundation. In the place of a world conforming to a single embracing order we discover that we must relate to each thing in its own light so that the former rigid order must yield to something more organic, fluid and creative, something that will allow for metaphor, ambiguity and paradox.

Inscape demands a change in the way we theorize about the world, a radical transformation in the order of our thought. But to discard this rigid form of logical consistency is not to abandon reason. Nature is clearly a coherent whole and our experiences, relationships, actions and interactions necessarily call for balance and harmony. What is required, therefore, is to drop the old fixed ways of thinking in favor of a new activity of integration; one that is open and organic yet no longer demands intellectual closure of the world. The challenge we now face is to discover that act of integration that will restore the balance between inner and outer, perception and action and create harmony between the individual and society, society and the environment; an integration that combines intellectual rigor and artistic creativity yet is no longer confined by the traditional demands of what could be called formal logic.

Rather than being the domain of science or philosophy these ideas of inscape and integration have been more generally explored by poets, writers and painters. Indeed, if we are to gain clues as to the perception and integration of inscape then one approach would be to look at works of art and at the different questions that painters have made manifest on their canvases.

Throughout the history of art, certain painters have constantly returned to their particular themes, subjects or motifs and explored them through different approaches, always questioning, never satisfied. For Monet, as he painted the facade of Rouen cathedral at different times of the day, he was engaging the subtle mystery of the way light gives life to the surface of an object. Cézanne returned again and again to Mont Ste-Victoire, that sail of white rock billowing high above the ochres and greens of the Provençal landscape. Picasso grappled with portraits of the women who, at different times of his life, served both as his companions and models, the energy of his perception never allowing him to rest. Again and again we see Picasso dissecting, rearranging, reintegrating, endlessly exploring his ambivalent relationship to the subject and object of his art.

Obsessed with this authenticity and inner mystery, an artist returns again and again to that act of perception and depiction, each time discovering new levels of truth, yet questioning how that truth is to be made manifest in line, form, mass, color, texture and so on. And so the artist moves both inward and outward, questions, engages and experiments. Not only artists but also poets and writers have returned to a particular theme in an attempt to unfold fresh elements of inner truth. Clearly, for the artist and the public alike, there can be no definitive interpretation of a work of art, no perfect reading of a poem.

In a similar sense, for a Native American elder there is no single authorized version of a creation story. Rather the story is ever fresh so that with each new telling, with each audience, season, ceremony and time of day the story is subtly different, revealing fresh insights. But there is always a definite order to the telling, a harmony that extends from night to night over the duration of the ceremony or season, a balance that affirms the life of the group and its relationship to the environment. But this order is not dominated by a simple logical connectivity or by an explicit consistency. Rather, it is a profoundly different order that grows out of a dynamical harmony and balance, an order of generation that is open and ever responsive.

The indigenous mind may well be able to tolerate paradox and ambiguity because this order is closer to the inner structure of reality than a more mathematical form of logic. This ambiguity is also expressed in the multileveled and multi-purposed nature of the telling itself. These are not stories in our modern western sense of anecdotes told for entertainment. They are part and parcel of the sacred; they are acknowledgements of creation, expressions of the consciousness of the group and its ancient history, celebrations of the land, subtle psychological lessons, education for children and harmonious ways of bringing people together. It is important to note, therefore, that the figure of the clown or joker occupies a privileged position within these stories. Indeed, the clown may also make his or her appearance during some of the sacred ceremonies. Again the Native American mind celebrates order and transformation, logic and paradox, the establishment of harmony and its subversion.

If our western science is to move beyond that sterility that views the world as object then it too must be willing to enter into new logical forms and new orders, orders that will tolerate ambiguity, paradox and metaphor, orders that give each experience a living space in which to move and to be, yet at the same time preserve the integrated balance of the whole.

I think that we can get some insight into how this can be done by looking at a painting, a still life by Cézanne, for example. Think of one of those many paintings in which a group of apples is arranged on a table. Clearly Cézanne does not begin with a fixed grid or schema into which each object must be fitted. Rather, each apple is engaged directly. By observing the marks left by Cézanne's brush we see how he questions the truth of his perception, constantly pushing the paint around, revising, making a tentative movement here, another there. Clearly this apple is no piece of dead fruit, no passive object placed in a landscape external to the artist. One could almost hazard that, during the act of painting, Cézanne had that same sense of the very aliveness of the apple, as does the Native American who says that a rock is alive. In both cases there is a direct engagement, a dialogue with nature.

But now Cézanne has moved to another region of the canvas and is engaged in a new and different manifestation of its essence. As ever he works tentatively, here on the apple, over there developing the pattern of the cloth, another apple, then back to the first. Pushing paint, describing the fragment of an outline, correcting the shade of a color, moving from region to region, never at rest, the painting never fully closed. And suddenly we realize that a totally new logic is at work, a totally new order of structuring. For the order of the canvas is emerging both out of the authenticity of each object in itself and the dynamic position that it occupies upon the canvas.

Contrast, for a moment, Cézanne's method with an Italian painting of the Renaissance in which the newly discovered device of perspective is being used. Perspective is that system whereby space, and the relationship between objects, is ordered according to a consistent mathematical scheme. In perspective the artist stands outside the scene and views landscape from a single, omnipotent position. All rays of light reach the eye of the painter and, in turn, each object must be transformed and distorted until it can fit the perspective grid. An apple close to the viewer must be made larger than one that is further away, the corner of a table is no longer a right angle, its sides cannot be portrayed as parallel. Rather than the shape of each object being seen in itself it is now depicted in a way that conforms to the overall demands of perspective.

Perspective, for such a painter, will not tolerate ambiguity or paradox since each object and each location in space must be made to conform to a pre-existing whole–even if that means distorting something of the inner truth of that object. The metaphorical connection between the painterly device of perspective and science's attempt to see the world as landscape so as to fit all experience into a single, consistent and logical pattern of thought will be obvious.

Clearly there would be a great deal of anxiety involved in letting go of such an all-embracing scheme. As long as the world is logical and consistent there is an unambiguous place for everything and there can be no room for uncertainty, paradox or irrationality. A consistent world appears to be a secure world, a world in which every relationship is well-defined. Yet ultimately such a world is dead and mechanical. It denies the vibrancy and paradox of life; it denies the openness of creativity and the very irrationality of being human. One's own honesty cannot allow one to remain in those peaceful waters of mechanical connectivity forever. With Cézanne, in particular, one senses that he was driven to question and never to be satisfied with any partial answer. For to let go of the dominance that traditional logic has over our thinking does not mean that we have given way to meaningless disorder. Rather, we are challenged to find new and deeper means of integration, to discover new orders that are alive and ever changing.

In Cézanne's case this attempt at integration was made from within the context of painting and its history. Cézanne was not simply concerned with the object as it presents itself in space but also with the problem of its representation on the surface of the canvas and with the different strategies whereby the viewer decodes this representation. Cézanne danced between observation and object, object and representation, representation and potential viewer. By constantly asking questions about the act of perception he forced us to engage his canvas and never find rest in a single all-embracing reading.

Unlike the academic painters of an earlier age, Cézanne was not going to be bound by the rules of perspective, in which the shape of each object is deformed according to the logic of a single consistent rule. Rather, he was seeking for a more organic order, one that would designate the strategies of perspective to their proper role within the act of painting. No longer does the corner of a table conform to the laws of perspective. An apple placed some distance from the painter may even appear larger than one close by, the plane of the table itself is dislocated and contours around an object no longer complete. Yet by relaxing his hold on earlier strategies Cézanne was able to achieve a much deeper integration within the whole painting, a means whereby the finished work can remain true to the inscape of his original vision.

The order of the work also mirrors the way in which Cézanne engaged in the act of painting; it is organic, unfolding, and embraces paradox, ambiguity and complementarity. Here he works in detail on an apple leaving some other portion of the canvas blank or lightly sketched. On the following day he focuses his attention upon some region of an apparently neutral background. And, as the painting progresses, he is constantly moving back and forth to apple, cloth, table, background. He tries to force a definite conclusion here but leaves something open there and poses a question somewhere else. Many days later a single brush stroke of blue in the background may force him to return to the apple and reopen its manifestation in a totally new way.

As I mentioned earlier, the art collector Ambroise Vollard has described the ardors of posing for Cézanne and how, after one hundred and fifteen sittings the painter declared, "The front of the shirt is not bad," but was still faced with the problem of painting in two small spots on the hands. In the end the painting was abandoned–moths had finally eaten through the sitter's clothes!

The new vision I am calling for would extend throughout all

phases of our lives and transform not only ourselves but also our society and its activities. Hand in hand with that transformation comes a new order of thought, a new way of integrating experience, perception and knowledge; one that combines intellectual rigor with creative openness; one that values harmony and balance over formal logic and surface consistency. It is not that human reason is to be thrown out of the window but that reason should be enriched by a new logic of perception, compassion, harmony and love.

This new order is closer to that of growth and creativity, closer to the evolution of a work of art rather than to that approach discussed earlier where knowledge is stretched to conform to the grid of logical consistency. It is worth noting that the most astounding of all creations of the human race, language, is ideally well adapted to deal with paradox, ambiguity, humor and complementarity. Indeed without this ability human communications would be reduced to something akin to the traffic of data between two computers.

As the worldview developed by western civilization continues to expand and dominate the planet it is clear that a profound change is called for. We can no longer continue to treat nature and human society as objects; we can no longer distance ourselves from our own humanity. If our planet is to survive, if society is to move towards health and if our own being is to be enriched then we must learn how to reach into life and embrace its very richness and paradox. We must strive for a new and fresher perception, a more harmonious form of action, and a different order to our society and its relationship to the environment.

RETURN TO PARI

Chapter 10

L ondon looked like being my home for the foreseeable future but chance was to intervene yet again. I was invited to a conference in Italy organized by Ervin Lazslo, the systems theorist. For old times sake we thought we would pass by Pari on the way to the conference and spend a night in the small local hotel. The following morning, while looking out of the window, we spotted Ferdinando, a teacher but also a writer and painter who had befriended us during our four-month stay in Pari. He shouted up to us and asked if we wanted a house. One of the women in the village had a house she was willing to rent for a year. We took a quick look and Maureen immediately said, "Yes." At the time I thought she was crazy. We were already renting an apartment in Blackheath. But Maureen pointed out that the house in Pari was very cheap to rent and we could always come back for the summer.

Back in London the time was coming up for us to renew our lease in Blackheath. This meant we were forced to engage in one of our very rare attempts at a balance sheet. The results were disturbing—we didn't have enough money to continue! When I used to read biographies about writers I wondered why they were always in debt and constantly writing letters in order to sponge off their friends. Now I knew why. You spend time working on a book proposal and send it to an editor who may or may not accept it. Eventually someone likes the idea and agrees to pay an advance–which finally appears in your bank account several months later. Now you have something to live off. A year or two later the book appears, but the advance has already been spent and you know you are not going to receive any royalties until that advance has first earned out. At this point when the unexpected occurs–a car repair, the need for new shoes, a computer that crashes, dental work–it has to be put on a credit card. Finally you begin to receive royalties but now you have credit card debts to pay off. And how big will the royalty check be? That is totally unpredictable. Book sales depend on so many factors such as reviews, word of mouth, fashion and the general economy. The whole thing is so variable that it is impossible for a writer to make financial plans. If you, gentle reader, have a position in a bank, office, business, factory or school then imagine what it would be like if your employer said that he wasn't going to pay you over the next few months but would try to make things up to you the following year–at the moment, though, it wasn't too clear as to what exactly he would be paying you!

Writing is a gamble that doesn't pay too well. Yet if you are a writer, or someone who explores ideas through books, then you just have to write. Someone asked Dylan Thomas why he wrote; "I'd be a damn' fool if I didn't!" was his reply.

Our financial position in London should have been obvious a year earlier. I simply thought that things would work out in a more positive way. I had high hopes that I would be able to write radio scripts for the BBC, as I had done for the CBC in Canada, but had not realized that the BBC was now contracting out most of its programming to small independent producers. I also had some disastrous news about my agent–or at least my former agent. For some time she had not been replying to my letters and e-mails and could not be reached by telephone. Now I found that my royalty statements and royalty checks were no longer arriving. It was only when I contacted some of her other clients that we realized that this had been happening to all of us. In some way money owing to us had been diverted to other ends. To this day I am still owed several years of royalty payments with no chance of that money ever being returned to me. On one occasion, while in France, I was asked to autograph one of my books that I was totally unaware had been translated—my agent had sold it and pocketed the money. With Gallic courtesy the owner signed it himself and presented it to me!

At all events we had to bite the bullet and agree that we could not survive in London. Our only hope was that little house in Pari. But before we finally left England there was one last thing to do—get back our original rental deposit. Despite phone calls and letters to the owner, getting our money back proved virtually impossible. It was at this point my photographer friend, Mark Edwards, explained a sure-fire method of getting any bill settled. "Just phone them and tell them you are a writer doing an article for a leading newspaper on, for example, flat rentals in London. Maybe someone in the office would like to comment on the matter of the return of a deposit for a David Peat?" It worked like a dream and a check arrived a few days later.

Moving meant that we had to go though our books yet again and make a selection of how many we could afford to ship to Italy. Finally in April 1996 we returned to Pari. The house we were renting was quite small and Maureen bemoaned the fact that the kitchen lacked a hot water tap. But that first year was peaceful. I read, painted, thought about things and began to work on another book. I also spent part of each day cooking and learned the local recipes by talking to the women in Pari as they waited in the shops or sat outside at night.

Pari has been around for centuries. Probably it had been a settlement in the time of the Etruscans who would have used the hot springs below the village. A map from 1250 shows the village much as it is today. Once Pari held a population of over a thousand, today there are just under two hundred inhabitants and people wonder what the ultimate fate of the village will be. Will it simply die out, with young people moving to work in the cities? Will the empty houses be bought up by tourists who only come for a week or two in the summer? Or is it possible that the village will revive, that artists and artisans will settle? Or will others arrive to carry out electronic work and yet others, tired of city life, work the land?

Pari is just one village out of thousands in Italy, France, Spain and other parts of the world. Maybe its long connection with the land is almost over. The photographer, Mark Edwards has been documenting peasant villages all over the world and feels they are the last dying remnant of a way of life that went back to the Neolithic age.

The people of Pari remain close to the land. Most families have a grove of olive trees, grape vines and a kitchen garden for their vegetables. In addition, some have fruit and nut trees, raise chickens and a pig that is killed around Christmas. Even those who now have a job in a bank or office still spend time on the land. As the months went on I began to realize there were similarities between life in Pari and the worldview of Native America. It seemed to me that much of Europe had once been like that. When *Blackfoot Physics* came to be republished I added a new chapter about the village of Pari. I also began to wonder where our modern society was going with its desire for constant progress and its obsession with control. It led me back to an idea I once had called *Gentle Action*. But more of that in the next excursion.

During our first years in Pari we remained observers to the life of the village. After all, we were triply strangers. We weren't Italian. We were not from the region of Tuscany and, finally, we were not born in a village where there are only a handful of family names that go back for centuries.

But then fate stepped in again. Following the meeting of artists and scientists in London an active debate began on the pages of my Web site. The discussion turned to the topic of education in general and the future of the universities in particular. Suddenly the possibility of funding another conference was proposed to me. At first I planned to run the conference in London or New York. But then I thought of the building at the top of the village—the former elementary school. Why not hold a meeting in the village of Pari?

Pari's village association is called *Sette Colli,* seven hills, and the ancient flag of Pari shows a group of hills with a carpenter's plane suspended above. The hills are the hills that surround Pari and the carpenter's plane indicates that one of these hills, the seventh, has been flattened. This is the hill on which Pari is located and indeed the top is flat—at one level. Hence the name of the village, for *pari* in Italian means "equal," "even" and "at one level." The original building on the top had been a castle but later was converted into a school and offices—there is even a dungeon underground!

When we first arrived in Pari the *"Palazzo"* as it was called, had been abandoned and its windows were broken. Then the *comune* decided to refurbish the ground floor and I realized it would make an excellent meeting place. I spoke to Tommaso Minacci, who was president of Sette Colli, and asked him if the village would like to host a conference. Suppose I handed him the check? The village would take care of all practical arrangements such as food and accommodation and I would be responsible for the academic side of things. Tommaso's first reaction was that they had no experience of such things or of hosting important people. "But you are all experts at running a *sagra* (a village festival)," I replied. "A conference would be no different."

And so in September of 2000, Pari's first international conference, "The Future of the Academy," was held with participants from Canada, USA, Austria, England, Portugal, Italy, France, Sweden and Australia. As soon as the meeting started it became clear that Pari had been an ideal choice. There was an excellent meeting room with oval table for twenty participants and several other rooms and offices. We could use the village meeting room as a dining hall, the local cooking was excellent and participants could be housed in the empty furnished houses. But what was more important, the meeting was being held in a village and not some anonymous hotel or conference center. People could walk around and enjoy the medieval setting and after dinner the local people could join us in singing together.

As to the meeting itself? There was a general feeling that contemporary universities were compromised in their function. Universities were supposed to be places of learning and teaching, they were repositories of knowledge, they were there to open young minds, encourage critical thinking, foster research and creativity. One participant suggested their traditional role had been to act as flywheels to damp the fluctuations of society. Yet in some cases contemporary universities appeared to be run by accountants and business managers who advertised for students and treated them as customers who demand a quick return for their money. Courses were not so much rated upon academic excellence but on how effective they would be in securing students a job. Participants spoke of the "orchid disciplines"–those subjects which, while of academic interest, did not offer a fast-track training to employment. Clearly such subjects could not be justified in a modern university. In fact the British Education Secretary, Charles Clarke, in a 2003 address at University College Worcester declared, "I don't mind there being some medievalists around for ornamental purposes, but there is no reason for the state to pay for them." He went on to proclaim that the state should fund only subjects of "clear usefulness."

In the context of the significant value of a university degree let me recall my student, David Schrum, who had flown to London shortly after completing his oral examination for his PhD. Some weeks later an envelope arrived from Canada with a customs declaration, "Degree Certificate. No Value"!

There was also the problem of increasing specialization and fragmentation of knowledge to the point where it was increasingly difficult for people to think and work within a broad spectrum. The participants also learned of so many cases in which a professor's promotion or salary increment would depend on how well they were rated by their students. How tempting it was to give an easy course with many students earning top marks.

All in all the conclusions of the meeting was rather depressing and since that time I have met quite a few university professors who dream of leaving their universities so that they can return to what first inspired them—research, writing, philosophical thinking and so on. By the final day participants felt that alternative "academies" were badly needed in the modern world, places where people could come to think and study, places were people could talk to each other across disciplines, academies that were not top heavy with administration and were not driven by profit motives. In fact there was a need for universities in the original sense of the word—somewhat informal communities where scholars could gather together. This is what happened when Peter Abelard left the cathedral of Notre-Dame and moved across the river to the left bank of the Seine. His students followed him and found lodgings nearby and in this way the University of Paris came into being.

So if there was a need for informal centers of learning and new academies why not Pari? I had been struck by the saying of the writer, Carlo Levi, "The future has an ancient heart." Pari had an ancient heart and it was also looking to the future. But first I had to find out what the people of Pari thought of the meeting. The answer came fairly quickly, "We enjoyed it as much as one of our village festivals. There were so many new faces around. Please run another conference."

And so the Pari Center for New Learning was born. The village and the local council of the surrounding villages gave us the use, without charge, of the conference room and offices in the *palazzo*. Over the next years we ran other international conferences, a series of courses and seminars and a visitors' program.

GENTLE ACTION AND GLOBAL SOLUTIONS

Excursion X

We are faced with problems of great complexity. The environment, society and even life on earth, is under threat and, as a result, the human race is struggling with feelings of anger, frustration and helplessness. Something, we urge, must be done; some action must be taken. Tomorrow, we sense, will be too late.

Yet it is these very feelings and reactions that have become part of the problem. The urge to change and control, to analyze, priorize, plan and act are all aspects of the same pattern that, in the first place, drove us to the edge of this crisis. What is needed is a radical change in human consciousness, in organizations and governments if we are to survive into the second half of the twenty-first century.

Civilizations and peoples of all historical periods, and all over the world, have made mistakes and behaved in unintelligent ways. (By intelligence I do not simply mean a sort of cleverness and an accumulation of knowledge. Rather wisdom, unprejudiced perception, clarity of mind, creativity and understanding are required.) The difference is that today's technology, weapons and global means of travel and communication are capable of magnifying our errors to the point that not only human life but also the ecology of the whole planet may be destroyed.

In the west, science and technology have made great strides

146

over the last two hundred years. These led to improvements in medicine, materials, new processes, travel and communications. But each advance has its accompanying drawbacks and unforeseen implications. Certainly it is true that some people must specialize in order to master the corner of a field of knowledge. But knowledge has also become associated with an attitude of fragmentation and what has been termed reductionism. While this world-view may have already been present in the psyche of the west from the thirteenth century, it has certainly been underlined by the triumphs of technology and the world-view of classical physics.

In spite of the many ecological, social and national problems that have surfaced in the last decades there still exists a strong belief that technology will be able to solve our difficulties, that issues can be analyzed in their particular domains and solutions can be proposed and implemented. We believe that it is possible for politicians and organizations to create adequate policies in response to the problems that face us and that the implications of a particular policy or course of action can be predicted in an objective way.

Yet the issues that face us today are vastly more complex and subtle than anything that science has attempted to tackle before. They include social, cultural, national and environmental dimensions that threaten the whole planet. Can technology and policy planning alone solve our dilemma or is something much deeper required, a change of consciousness perhaps, one that is accompanied by a more profound insight into our human nature?

What could be called the traditional Newtonian, or mechanical, approach oversimplifies, fragments and very often leaves out what is most important. In addition, its power to make models, precise calculations, and come up with predictions far into the future, lures us into the false sense of security that we actually know what we are doing. Two hundred years of scientific analysis and prediction has encouraged our objectification of the world, an objectification that has the effect of neglecting human values and weakening our relationship to nature. This approach enhances our tendency to dominate, control and exploit the natural world. Every problem, it is believed, has a solution that can be applied to a particular part of the system. And if that solution does not work, then yet another study group must be convened and its proposals applied with even greater vigor. Objectifying nature leads to a loss of sensitivity and to a lack of meaning at our living and being in the world.

When I was a student I drove an old car with the disconcerting tendency to come to a sudden shuddering halt in remote locations. But in those days I also had a pamphlet that helped me figure out what had gone wrong. This diagnostic sheet began by breaking down symptoms to determine if the problem lay in the fuel supply or the electrical system. If no fuel was reaching the engine, for example, did the fault lie between the fuel tank and the carburetor? Step by step the source of the failure could be traced to an individual component. On one occasion it turned out to be a blocked needle valve, on another moisture in the distributor cap. By dividing the car into a series of separate parts and taking into account the interconnections between them it was possible to make a correct diagnosis of any problem and take the necessary action. Getting the car running again involved cleaning, repairing or replacing the part that proved faulty.

When it comes to engines and machines this approach is extremely powerful. It allows a complex system to be analyzed into a series of separate interacting parts in which the solution to any malfunction focuses on a particular faulty component. Machines can be analyzed in this way and the outcome of any intervention can be predicted. How simple it would be if the same technique could be applied to the global problems that face us today—to economics, ecology, human conflict and even to our bodies. The difference is that nature, society and human beings are not machines but are enormously more complex and subtle so that their behavior cannot be analyzed, evaluated or predicted in any mechanical way.

Our everyday experience tells us that nature is very definitely not mechanical, nevertheless in so many ways we continue to behave as if it were. If we view nature and society as some sort of highly sophisticated machine then we tend to act and treat it in a mechanical way and that is where the trouble lies. Our organizations often react in these ways and legislators believe that all problems have well-defined solutions, that every situation can be exhaustively analyzed and that the outcome of a course of action can be accurately predicted. That, in essence, is why the world faces so many problems today and why the solutions offered by organizations and governments often do not work or end up making a situation much worse.

If, at its deepest level, the world is not mechanical yet our strategies and plans continue to be predicated upon a mechanical perspective, then we are in serious trouble. Mistaking the red light of a stop signal for a neon advertising sign may lead to a traffic accident. But looking at the problems of a rain forest, inner city violence, or the human body as if they are readily analyzable and would yield solutions with predictable outcomes is going to land us in even deeper trouble. Perceiving and valuing nature in inappropriate ways has brought us into the crisis the whole planet now faces.

The problem lies in our inadequate perception of the world and our lack of any proper relationship to nature. This has become entrenched in our institutions, social values and policies. The world is an organic, living thing, flexible and ever-changing yet the institutions we have created to deal with it are all too often rigid and insensitive. Our policies are so often reactive and persist long after the context in which they were created has changed. Hierarchical organizations that have limited lines of communication and inflexible inner structures are supposed to deal with a rich and complex world. How is it possible for any policy to meet the challenges of a system that is far more subtle and varied than the institution that attempts to control it? Such intervention is doomed to failure. Science and technology are not going to save the world, neither are computer models and policy studies. What is needed is something radically different that is at least as subtle as the issues and natural systems we face.

Is there a way out? How can we deal with systems so complex and sensitive that they defy the most advanced computer? I believe that each one of us possesses the tool to do the job—the human brain, a brain moreover that is an integral part of a sensing, feeling, human body. Institutions may be the dinosaurs of the modern world, yet they are composed of human beings who think and feel and are born with the capacity for unlimited creativity. The question, therefore, is how can our human creativity, values, thoughts and feelings restore harmony on our planet and give greater meaning to our relationship with each other and the world?

The point about creativity and, indeed, about being alive is that it cannot be prescribed; it is ever-changing and ever-new. Certainly a creative response cannot be laid down as a fixed program in a book. Nevertheless I would like to point to certain clues and signposts, the first of which is to look at the possibility of doing nothing, or as I prefer to put it, an active and creative suspension of action.

Our modern world is founded on the desire for endless progress and novelty. When in doubt, do something. When faced with a problem, look for a solution and apply it. When a crisis threatens our natural reaction is to act. We call upon our governments to take action. But doing something got us into this mess in the first place and can lead to unpredictable consequences. What happens, however, if an organization decides to suspend action?

Of course the lights will begin to flash and the alarm bells ring. Like Pavlov's dog an organization is conditioned to react and respond. But what if it does nothing–but in a very watchful way (and this applies not only to organizations but to individuals as well)? The first stage will be one of panic and chaos, a flow of commands and information. All of this is not being generated by any external threat but through the internal structure of the organization itself. By remaining sensitive to what is going on it may be possible to become aware of the whole nature of the organization, of its values, the way its information flows, its internal relationships, dynamics and, in particular, its fixed and inflexible responses–the organizational neuroses and psychoses if you like.

Arthur Koestler suggested that a scientific revolution is born out of the chaos produced when a paradigm breaks down. It is possible that something new and more flexible could be born out of the breakdown of fixed patterns in an organization, policy group or individual. By means of a very active watchfulness it may be possible to detect its unexamined presuppositions, fixed values and conditioned responses and in this way allow them to dissolve by no longer giving energy to support them. The idea would be to permit the full human potential for creativity within each individual to flower, it would enable people to relate together in a more harmonious way and human needs and values to be acknowledged.

The type of action or remedy that is required will, of course, vary from situation to situation, which suggests that a policy or organization itself should not be fixed but must evolve organically with changing contexts, continually dying to its fixed forms and being born anew. In some cases intervention may be directed towards a particular problem but in others a global and gentle form of action may be needed. Ecologies, economies and human societies are fundamentally holistic, with the result that influences at one location propagate throughout the systems. Moreover they are extraordinarily sensitive to certain types of change so that what is required is not some major intervention but something very gentle and delicate. The problem of an oil spill may suggest an immediate clean-up in a particular location, but preserving the Brazilian rain forests requires a more subtle form of action that begins, not simply in the forest itself, but in locations as distant as Japan and the US and involves activity in a host of different fields such as trade, economics, agriculture and ethics.

What I am calling *gentle action* can be applied globally as it seeks to restore harmony. To return to a mechanistic example, it could be compared to the fine-tuning of an automobile in which a series of tiny, coordinated adjustments allow for greater power and efficiency. Another example is to contrast it with the violent local action of a stone thrown in a lake from which ripples spread out until they are lost in the tiny random wavelets at the edge. Suppose, however, that a harmonious coordination of tiny waves at the edge of the lake were possible. This would require a non-local yet gentle action that flows from a much greater sensitivity to the whole system. Surprising though it may seem, physics shows that if such coordination is made of all the phases of the individual wavelets then these ripples will begin to interfere with each other in a constructive way. They start to move inward, towards the middle of the lake and grow in size until they produce a splash right in the center. In an amazing fashion a large effect is produced out of a very gentle action involving the whole of the lake. A great flow of energy has grown organically out of a highly intelligent yet almost imperceptible form of intervention.

THE PARI CENTER FOR NEW LEARNING

Chapter 11

It is really impossible to place a boundary around what we do here in Pari. It really makes no sense to say, "This is a village activity," "That is a Pari Center activity," or even "This is a family activity." Each one of these merges into the others. An activity of the Pari Center may help the village in some practical way. In turn, the very presence of the village is of advantage to the Pari Center. And as to the family…? Some years ago our daughter, Eleanor, left Canada to work in London but then came to Pari, first on a visit and then to live.

At the time we were not the only strangers to come to the village. Another new resident was Carlo Barbieri who came from Como in the north of Italy. He had bought a farm to run as an *agriturismo* (a farmhouse that takes in guests). One day, Carlo's son, Andrea, by some pre-existing schema came down to Pari to visit his father. He met my daughter and that evening they went for a walk together, not returning until around four in the morning.

Andrea was only in Pari for a few days, as he had to return to Como where he worked as a freelance graphic designer. Several days later Eleanor received a phone call from him telling her he was about to visit an old girlfriend. At the same moment Eleanor heard the front doorbell ring. She went downstairs to find Andrea with his cell phone in his hand. He had returned with his computer to live in Pari. And now we have three grandchildren living in the village who are constantly dropping in. Maureen's son, Marcel, came on a flying visit some years ago while touring Europe and he also decided to settle in the village, working as a Web site designer. (I should add that both Maureen's mother and mine died in Pari and are buried in the cemetery, so there are now four generations of us in the village!)

Pari is ideally placed as a center. Siena is only thirty-five km to the north and Florence is an hour from Siena. Other day trips take visitors to Assisi, Pisa, Orvieto and Arezzo. Nearby, there is the grave of San Galgano, a twelfth century knight who plunged his sword into a rock–the sword-in-the-stone can still be seen today and the saint's name may well be a variant of that of Gawain. Indeed, the names Merlino and Arturo appear in parish registers during that period–a time before the first Arthurian legends had been written down. Legend has it that the nearby monastery of Sant' Antimo, was founded by Charlemagne. And Sant' Antimo itself is near to Montalcino–the center for the famous Brunello wines. Drive south of Pari and you come to Roselle–the remains of an Etruscan city. A little further south and you come to a provincial park on the shores of the Mediterranean, a favorite place for a day trip in summer.

Here in Pari we watch the seasons go by. Planting takes place according to the moon; otherwise the parsley will not come up! In summer it is too hot to work in the fields by around 10:30 in the morning, but there is always a breeze after sunset, which makes it possible to sleep at night. October sees the start of the rain and then the *vendemmia*–picking the grapes and making wine. After this it is time to pick the olives and bring them to the *frantoio*–the olive press in the village. During that period the entire village is filled with the odor of olive oil.

The new oil is yellow and thick, with a slightly spicy taste. The best way to enjoy it is to rub garlic on a piece of toasted Tuscan bread and then pour the oil over. It is also used to give a baptism to soups such as *ribollita*. As the winter arrives and the colder weather sets in the oil changes to a clear green color and the flavor becomes milder. Analysis of the oil indicates that not only is it good for reducing cholesterol but it contains anti-oxidants that prevent free-radicals, one of the causes of aging. Olive oil, a diet of fresh foods, meat from game or animals that are allowed to graze in fields and the absence of stress is probably the reason that the inhabitants of Pari live to extreme old age. If someone happens to die in their late seventies the locals would say, "Poor thing, he (or she) was no age."

But back to the Pari Center for New Learning. Following the success of our first meeting in 2000 we decided to run other conferences–on the applications of chaos theory in society, on the future of knowledge and publishing in the world of the Internet, on religion and science. We also decided to offer week-long courses.

The Center received funding to run a series of talks on science and spirituality and is a three-time winner of the Metanexus Institute's prize awarded for "organizational excellence and creative programming." This activity of combining science and spirituality came about in the following manner–another example of the way in which chance opens a door. A few years ago I was invited to the architecture department of the University of Madrid to give a lecture and spend the week looking at the work of the students. Maureen and I arrived in Madrid and on the following day I gave my talk. I spoke in English but the talk was translated into Spanish. At some point I introduced the ideas of David Bohm and noticed how attentive the audience had become. After the talk one of the students said how amazed they were that a pop singer should have such profound ideas about physics. It was at this point I learned that the name David Bohm had been translated as David Bowie!

At the end of the talk my host broke the news that a strike had just been announced at the university. I would still be their guest for the week but would not be able to come into the university. On impulse Maureen and I took the train to Córdoba where we learned of that special time in El Andalus when Jews, Christians and Muslims worked together, translated each other's books and studied arithmetic, astronomy, medicine and botany side by side. It was the Arabs who brought the new learning into Europe and Córdoba became one of the most important centers in the Western world. Tragically this era did not persist for, with the conquest of Córdoba in 1236 by King Ferdinand III, the area became a Catholic base. Subsequently Jews and Muslims were given the choice of conversion or exile.

The spirit of that period touched us deeply and Maureen said, "We should be doing this in Pari," and so we organized a conference entitled "A Dialogue between Jews, Christians, Muslims and Science." We had hoped to get funding from a certain source but after the tragedy of the Twin Towers on September 11, 2001 it was, for one funding body at least, a politically sensitive issue to have Christians, Jews and Muslims at the same table. And so our expected funding did not materialize and we were faced with the question that has always guided us in Pari. "Should we be doing this?" "Is this the right thing to do?" If it *is* the right thing then we should go ahead and do it–even if the funding is not in place. (In this respect I should add that when, previously in Canada, Maureen and I had started a little business involving writing, she decided to call it "Mr Micawber Associates," naming it after the figure in *David Copperfield* who, as an eternal optimist, declared that "Something will turn up.")

And so we ran the meeting and brought new faces to Pari. The day after the meeting one of the participants, Therese Schroeder-Sheker, mentioned the Metanexus Institute and how they funded local groups to run talks on religion and science. We looked them up on the Internet and discovered that this very day happened to be the deadline for applications. Therese and I worked all evening on the application and submitted it before midnight. We were delighted to learn, some weeks later, that we had been successful.

Thus began a series of talks, in Italian, on various aspects of science and religion. We also ran more conferences. One included Romel George Ziadeh, a representative from Habitat Jordan. In the evenings Romel sat in the piazza smoking his hookah and offering smoke to people in the village.

After we formed the Pari Center I decided to offer courses and workshops. The first was a one-week overview of ideas in modern physics with language, logic, perception and paradigms thrown in for good luck. Later I added "Synchronicity: The Bridge between Matter and Mind," and in 2004, "Art, Science and the Sacred."

I really enjoy teaching these courses—a small group of us all living in the same tiny village for a week, eating together and sitting around a table to talk. I generally begin around 10:00 in the morning until 12:30. Then lunch, a siesta and back again from 4:00-6:30 or 7:00 followed by dinner. By the fourth day most participants have become mentally exhausted so we have a free day when they can visit Siena or walk in the surrounding countryside or just relax.

I never plan these courses in any great detail but have a large series of topics from which I can draw depending on the overall interest of the group. In turn these topics are not mapped out in detailed notes but consist of a series of headings to remind me of the logical flow. What amazes me about these courses is how something new always seems to emerge. I can be speaking about a topic I know very well but suddenly I say something that simply staggers me. I have to go back and repeat it—it is an idea that never occurred to me before and the first thing I do is to thank the participants because somehow their interest and attentiveness have created something new—a gift of insight. I should add that something similar sometimes happens when I write—I discover I have written something that I didn't previously know.

Certainly I never think that *I* have written the book. In fact over the past months I have been absent-mindedly referring to this present book as a "biography" rather than an autobiography. It is as if I am writing about the life of someone called David Peat. Does this make any sense to you, the reader? Arnold Smith, who spent two years at the Pari Center, often remarked that there are two separate characters—one who walks around Pari and talks to people and someone quite distinct who writes the books with the name F. David Peat on the cover. I certainly would agree that the author of these books is a great deal smarter than I am!

But back to the courses. Nearly every group is cohesive and exhibits a particular characteristic—even though the individuals have never met before. "This is the most serious group you have ever had, David. What's the matter with them?" the cooks may say. Or " We can't get them out of the room at night, they're always talking and joking and they eat everything we put in front of them." Other groups eat little but drink a great quantity of wine. Some groups love to ask questions and get into discussions to the point where I feel I can lean back and let them get on with it. Others constantly demand more: more facts, more ideas, and more explanations. They can be pretty exhausting!

While our main courses are given in English we have also begun to offer more events in Italian. I well remember a long weekend I gave to a group of *notai*. A *notaio* has a particular legal function in Italy and is very influential. They are a little like a notary public, in that they draw up legal documents—for example, the transfer of property—but also have a very important role when new laws are to be considered. The group had invited me to speak because they believed that the Italian legal system had become increasingly fragmented. The vision of wholeness embraced by quantum theory, as well as by self-organized systems would serve as a powerful metaphor. And so in addition to quantum jumps and quantum healing we may have quantum law!

Not all my teaching takes place in Pari because I get invited to give talks and attend conferences in Europe and the USA. Generally it seems like a good thing at the time to agree to attend but as the date to travel approaches I ask myself–do I really want to leave Pari? Do I really want to sit on a plane for ten hours and suffer jet lag? On the other hand there is something about remaining in the public eye. If people are going to buy my books then it is a good idea to make the occasional appearance in Britain or the US. I can also use the opportunity to talk to people about the Pari Center and renew contact with old friends. And so I generally say, "Yes" and turn up on time. But there have been notable exceptions. Once I was invited to talk to members of Centromarca–the association of Italian brand names–in Milan. I arrived the day before and checked into the luxury hotel they had booked for me. On noting the enormous bathtub I decided to soak and relax. While I was drifting in the hot water, the phone rang–in a hotel such as this one there was a phone in the bathroom. It was the conference organizer on the line. I told him I had arrived and everything was on schedule for the following afternoon. "But you speak today," he told me. "You are on in half an hour." But by the time I had dried, dressed and found my way to the meeting room I was too late.

Then there was the time I didn't speak at the Eranos conference in Switzerland. Getting to Eranos meant a bus to Florence, a train to Milan and then change for the train going towards Zurich. Unfortunately the trains from Florence were running very late that day. I arrived in Milan and started to run towards the departures board when I heard an announcement–and naturally in any country these mechanically distorted voices are hard to understand–but this one definitely said "Zurich," gave a platform number and said, "About to depart." I ran, waved to the conductor and jumped on the train. I was very much out of breath but eventually settled down and turned to my neighbor. "This is going to Zurich, isn't it?" "No," he replied, "We're going to Rome. This train is *coming* from Zurich." And so I arrived back at my starting point—Florence—after midnight.

Do we have time for one more story? I was to speak at a conference in France and so Maureen and I left several days in advance in order to stop at one of our favorite places in France, Menton, which is just on the border with Italy. By coincidence I am writing these present paragraphs in a small apartment overlooking the Menton harbor. Menton was once part of the Principality of Monaco. It faces south and is surrounded by a bay of hills, which keeps it warm in the winter. In fact Menton has more hours of sunshine than any other location in France. Today, 20 November for example, we have just eaten lunch in the town sitting in the sun at an outdoor café.

As we happen to be in France for a few paragraphs, I should perhaps recommend another French town, Tournus on the river Saône in the Burgundy wine region. It contains the Abbey of Saint-Philibert, which Renoir felt was an outstanding example of French architecture.

But back to that earlier visit to Menton. We walked the ancient streets, enjoyed the view of the sea and learned that many English people, suffering from tuberculosis, had settled in the town and are buried in the cemetery. Katherine Mansfield, the New Zealand writer, had spent extended periods in Menton hoping for a cure for her TB. It was a town favored by Jean Cocteau and has a museum devoted to his art. After paying a visit to see his paintings and ceramics we both felt that he should have focused more on his filmmaking. Several days later I realized I should be on my way to the conference. But after driving for a few hours I began to ask myself: Do I really want to sit in a room with a lot of people and listen to talks? And so we turned the car back towards the sea and found a cabin on the beach at a little town called Agay. Returning to the sea turned out to have been an important decision because, on the following day, as I sat on the beach with my notebook, the whole theme and content of my next book came to me. After only two days the entire book was more or less mapped out.

ETHICS AND ACTIONS

Excursion XI

Earlier I wrote of our meeting with the Blackfoot. At that time one of them asked David Bohm to explain superconductivity.

"It is a state of extreme order," Bohm replied.

"But everything in nature is in balance so if there is order in one place there must be disorder in another," the elder observed.

Bohm smiled. "Yes, that is correct. The disorder is called entropy."

"Then are you morally responsible for the disorder you create?"

We were taken aback. That was something we had not expected to hear. Certainly scientists discuss the moral responsibility involved in developing a new weapon and doctors talk about the ethical issues involved in genetic manipulation but to suggest that there was an ethical and moral dimension to building a superconductor was a different matter altogether.

On the other hand where do ethics end and where does objective science begin? Where do our personal actions cease and our collective social interactions commence? Can any boundaries be drawn? One thing we have learned in the twentieth century is the hubris inherent in science. After the testing of the atomic bomb Oppenheimer said, "Now science knows original sin." Likewise Wolfgang Pauli spoke of "the will to power" inherent in modern science.

Chaos theory has exploded the illusion of our desire for absolute certainty and total predictability. Many of nature's systems are able to spontaneously organize themselves and, in so doing, generate their own laws and patterns of behavior. Natural systems can enter chaotic phases or phases of such enormous complexity that they lie beyond the ability of the largest of computers to describe these systems exhaustively. This means that there will be serious limitations on our ability to understand with total certainty the long-range impacts of our actions, beliefs and perceptions.

Once, in the Newtonian era, we saw the world as a giant mechanism composed of interlocking parts. Such machines can be analyzed in logical, rational ways. Their errors can be traced to particular defects that can then be repaired or replaced. This dream of the power of rationality persists–the dream that nature and human society can be controlled by scientific analysis and the application of ever more technology. But what if that world outside is far more subtle and complex than the tools of our analysis?

We may think we know about "the war on terror," but do we know where the seeds of terrorism arise? We read of famine and civil war but can we comprehend how our particular belief systems, isolated in the industrial world, impact on a small Third World country? Do we really understand the origins of poverty and ignorance? And so we are forced to ask: how can we act ethically and morally with respect to the world around us?

It may be comforting to believe that we will always act as ethical individuals, but what particular ethical system is going to guide us? Ethics are not universal. They may be founded on tradition, taboos or particular religions. Western society, for example, combined the Judeo-Christian ethic with the fruits of Greek philosophy.

So what of ethical philosophers? Can they guide us? It turns out that, at best, most of them can only provide tools for analysis of particular situations rather than rules for behavior. They may enquire, as did Plato, if ethics is based upon universal principles encoded into the fabric of the universe. Or, following Aristotle, if they are the natural actions of good people. Kant on the other hand suggested that ethics are to be learned and lead us to duties that must be carried out. The Utilitarians, John Stuart Mill and Jeremy Bentham, did not feel that personal motives or guiding principles were as important as simply calculating which actions would produce the greatest happiness to the greatest number of people. In short ethics could be positioned anywhere along that spectrum that leads from principles to actions, or from results and implications.

Our present dilemma is simple yet paradoxical; our world is badly in need of ethical principles that can be agreed upon by all–by individuals of different histories, religions and cultures, and by corporations and governments. The recent scandals in the business world suggest that we also need guidelines that enable corporate behavior to become more regular and predictable. In this way uncertainty will be reduced and the threat of economic chaos or collapse avoided. If this does not happen then we are all going to suffer–rich and poor, industrial nation and Third World farming community alike. Yet where are we to look for such principles?

Science and its associated technology have made enormous advances over the last century and, at the same time, presented us with situations involving serious moral and ethical dilemmas–genetic engineering, global warming, the technology of war, mass communications, human fertility–the list goes on and in each case there are serious ethical decisions to be made. But by whom? By scientists? Politicians? Academics? Or the general public?

I was once told the following story. Following the assassination of Gandhi, Nehru sought out Jiddu Krishnamurti and asked him what he should do as the leader of his nation. "Right action," was the reply. In one way this may appear over-simplistic yet in another it seems to be exactly right. That is something we have attempted to practice in Pari by asking the questions, "Is this the right thing to do?" "Is this something we should be doing at this moment?"

Yet what happens when we face systems and situations that are so incredibly complex that we can never know the consequences of our actions? Maybe what seems right at the time may have unforeseen long-term effects. Maybe taking no action will minimize damage or maybe a sudden intervention is desperately needed. So again we ask what can we do?

I find I have no answers and that bothers me. Our world does need guidelines but where are we to find them? Maybe there is one thing we can do and that is to look at nature's systems in the world around us.

Many natural systems can be remarkably robust and persist for centuries and millennia. They repair themselves, they face challenges, and they adjust. The buffalo roamed the North American plains long before the first Europeans arrived. But then, when the prairies were converted to a wheat bowl, shorter-rooted crops replaced the deep-rooted buffalo grass and gradually the surface soil was blown away by the winds. Nature had found a way to contain and preserve an environment; human intervention destroyed that delicate balance.

Likewise forests endure, they survive fires, the rise and fall of insect populations and fluctuations in rainfall. They, and so many other ecologies, do this because they have evolved what, from the outside, we could perhaps describe as a set of principles.

Nature's systems organize themselves and survive because something is always flowing through them—it could be energy, it could be the flow of matter, and when it comes to human systems it could also be the flow of information. Take forests, as an example. Energy flows through the forest in the form of sunlight. Matter enters in the form of water from rain and oxygen from the air. What is more, as this energy and matter move through the system they are shared out and transformed in multiple ways. Natural systems survive because of the enormous number of what are called feedback loops–multiple interconnections if you like.

Another criterion is multiplicity and diversity, which implies a respect for completion. If one plant or species seeks to squeeze out all others then biodiversity becomes impoverished. The Irish Potato Famine was brought about because farmers were instructed to grow only one crop–potatoes. When disease hit and the potato crop was destroyed there was nothing else to take its place. Yet in nature, if particular plants, animals or insects fall prey to disease there will always be others that will take their place and preserve an ecological balance. Competition also ensures that no single entity grows too big to compromise the health of the whole. In fact the survival of any one species depends upon the survival of the whole. Large corporations should learn this lesson, that the key to survival lies in their ability to foster the health of the market as a whole. This means there must be reciprocity and cooperation between every element of an ecology or an economy.

Those in the business world are always thinking of efficiency, yet, according to their criteria, nature is anything but efficient for it is always doing the same thing in a multiplicity of different ways. Nature is filled with redundancy and duplication. On the face of it this may look inefficient, but when situations change, or damage occurs, there will always be other parts of the system that can take over. Block a major blood vessel in the leg and other smaller vessels take over the job of transporting blood. And which of us would fly in a totally efficient airliner that had no back-up systems?

Is there a lesson here? Could these guidelines and principles suggest to us ways of acting that could be called ethical? If so they would be as follows:

a) Foster Transparency and Openness

Natural systems survive because of their rich network of feedback loops. In this way, for example, nutrients are shared and flow through the system. Animals, plants, insects and bacteria grow and die, but even when they are dead they provide food for others. By sharing in a vast web of interlocking systems each part contributes to the whole and the whole supports each part.

b) Respect for the Whole

Organizations and businesses may try to grow bigger and bigger but in the end they will only prosper if the economy is healthy and the business community as a larger whole is able to survive through a measure of trust and confidence. This can only happen when each individual player realizes that his or her survival depends upon the health of the whole. Therefore each has an obligation to support that whole. Even when elements of a system are in competition they are at the same time contributing to the well-being of that system as a whole. Likewise a corporation is nourished by the market and those around it—suppliers, customers and even competitors. Maintaining the health of the entire system is the ethical obligation of each corporation to the whole.

c) Respect for Competition

Natural systems flourish because of their inherent diversity. If any one species became too big and started to dominate the system then that environment would decline. Competition is necessary to keep an ecosystem flexible with multiple feedback loops and pathways whereby energy and matter or, in the case of human society, goods, money and information can flow.

d) Acknowledge Redundancy

Nature tends to achieve the same end in a number of different ways. It is important for us to realize this in daily life and acknowledge that maximizing efficiency could make us over-rigid and incapable of making quick adjustments when the market changes.

e) Respect Creativity

Charles Darwin remarked that the most important agent in an entire ecology is the humble earthworm that spends much of the day searching for food and, in so doing, is constantly turning over and aerating the earth. Likewise every organization and society contains people who have their own natural creativity and skills. Some are earthworms, others dragonflies. By offering each one respect it will be possible to draw on their inherent creativity. When we are respected, each one of us feels a greater sense of responsibility and are able to unleash creativity at all levels.

f) Accepting Uncertainty

Uncertainty and limits to control are facts of life that must be accepted within any non-linear system. There will always be a degree of "missing information" which at times can make us uncomfortable. Likewise we may not always be able to control what occurs around us. The result depends on whether we view this in terms of insecurity and lack of control or in terms of a door into new possibilities and relationships.

CONCLUSIONS

Chapter 12

When we first arrived in Pari there were many empty but furnished houses–houses belonging to an uncle, cousin or some other family member who had died or moved to a city. At first it was difficult to rent one of these–no one really had the concept of renting out property. We first rented a tiny house from Rosita and then, in 2001, moved to a larger house that faced south and caught the sun so that it was possible to sit out on the small balcony in January and February. Our daughter, Eleanor, also began by renting with her husband Andrea. Next, Maureen's son, Marcel arrived and looked for somewhere to live. Gradually people began to be open to the idea of renting for long periods.

The next step was short-term rentals. As the Center became established, people wrote to ask if they could visit. We have had people here from anything from a week or two to several months. They come to study, to write or to talk with others at the Pari Center. Elisabet Sahtouris spent time here to write a book on the earth as Gaia and Maggie Calloway was working on her new book *The Energetics of Business*. Ros Murray, an artist from Ireland, made an installation in the *palazzo*. Both Ray Sczawinski and Philip Franses spent two extended periods in Pari before moving to Schumacher College and taking a master's degree. The end result was that more and more houses were being rented on both a short- and long-term basis.

A high point was the visit of the Liverpool Pub Philosophers. This was a group who met on a regular basis in a Liverpool pub to discuss philosophy. During their visit they drank all the beer in Pari's local bar as well as beating the village 10-6 at soccer.

Arnold Smith, who was involved in Artificial Intelligence research in Canada, spent two years with the Center and said that he had met more interesting and stimulating people who passed through Pari than he had ever met in a large city. Our associate director, Shantena Sabbadini, was a theoretical physicist working on the quantum measurement problem and the physics of black holes before spending time at an ashram in India. Back in Italy he became involved in running the Jungian conferences at Eranos in Switzerland as well as making a new translation of the *I Ching*. Shantena settled in a village not far from Pari and amongst other things helps to organize our dialogues on religion and science.

All this activity means that visitors and participants at courses and conferences are spending money in the village, at the local shops and in the restaurants and bar, as well as paying rent. And when it comes to courses and conferences we usually hire local cooks and maybe a cleaner and driver. This money is flowing through the village but I have no idea what effect this has. I don't really know in what ways it circulates or what role it could play in the future of the village or even if it could lead to new forms of work for the young people. These I think are questions that only an economist or a sociologist may be able to answer. One thing I do know, however, is that every event has had a definite social impact. For example, the last event of 2006, the course "Art, Science and the Sacred," ended in October. A few days later I went into the local shop to hear people saying, "It's sad, there will be no new faces around until next year."

The community of Pari has been around for centuries and, from listening to the local people I gather that, until the 1950s, it functioned in ways that were relatively unchanged. Historically Pari used a barter system and there was very little money in circulation. What money there was came from the sale of wine to Siena or by smuggling salt past a nearby customs post in order to avoid the salt tax imposed by the Papal States. (Italian tobacconists to this day have a sign with a T outside their shops indicating the tax on tobacco and salt.)

The people of Pari did not need cash in their pockets because the land provided everything. There was stone for building houses. Large deposits of clay are to be found near Siena and were made into bricks in the village. There were copper and iron mines within walking distance. Wood was used as fuel and made into charcoal for cooking. The local blacksmith worked in wrought iron. (Today Siro recalls the way he joined two pieces of metal, not with an oxy-acetylene torch, but by hammering the hot metal together. He also made shoes, not for horses but for the bullocks that pulled the plows and the bullock carts.)

Wheat fields provided flour for bread, and a watermill ground the wheat. In every kitchen there was a *madia*–a wooden chest with a lid that, when raised, exposed a place for storing the ingredients and an area for making the bread. Early in the morning the loaves were taken to one of the public wood-fired ovens.

The stalks of the *ginestra*, or broom plant, were cut and placed under the hot sulfurous water of the Petriolo spring, located just below the village. After several days fibers could be extracted from the plant, spun and woven into towels, bed linen and sacks for olives. Sheep provided wool and since there were mulberry trees around maybe even silk was made. The shoemakers of the village made sandals out of snakeskin and shoes from leather.

At that time people were poor, indeed the Tuscans were called the "bean eaters," their only meat coming from what they could hunt in the woods–wild boar, deer, hare, pheasants and songbirds. And songbirds brings me to a story about Remo, a local musician who sadly died a few years ago. Remo was quite old when he received a visit from an American woman who was also a professional musician. Remo showed her the musical instruments he used to play, and the collection of birdcalls he had carved. He explained that he used to be keeper of the local reservoir and how he would call to the birds. Patiently he explained about each bird and the call it made.

"I would call to them and they would reply and gather around my feet."

The visitor's eyes lit up at this saintly man, a sort of reincarnation of St Francis of Assisi. "How wonderful!"

"Yes, it was," Remo replied, "because then I could catch them and eat them."

Let me relate another story that happened in Pari as well as in many other Italian villages during the war. Three families of Jews (Poles and Russians) arrived in Pari, fleeing the Nazis. For a time they were given food and shelter in local houses. But when the village learned that the Gestapo was on its way, the families were taken to the shacks of charcoal burners who lived in the woods. In the event that one of the villagers might be caught and questioned, the priest decided that he alone would know the exact location of each family. He would take them food and, when the Allied bombardment of Pari began and the charcoal burners returned to their families, he became their only lifeline. The Jewish families survived the war and one family returned some years later to thank the local people. In the cemetery the priest's grave is still tended by people who remember him and his heroic behavior.

While electricity came to the village in the 1930s, there was no running water and Pari had to rely on its two wells until the fifties. The women used a trough at the entrance to the village to do the family wash. This also meant that there were no flush toilets which was not too bad because ordure was used to fertilize the land. There is an amusing story to that effect. Sometimes ordure was stored in wine casks to be transported to the olive groves and vineyards. As the liberating Allied forces moved up from the south they passed Pari, saw barrels of what they assumed to be wine and stole them. The villagers were saddened by the loss of their fertilizer but were amused to think of the faces of the liberators when they learned the true contents of the barrels.

In those days the people of Pari reached the city of Siena either by bullock cart or on foot. Before the building of the present superstrada, this meant a long meandering trek through several of the small villages in the area. This was not a return trip that could be done in a day but required a person to spend the night in Siena before returning. (One man told me of how he used to sleep on a table in a bar.) Then, some time in the 1950s or '60s, the first car appeared in Pari. Now it became possible to make the round trip to Siena in a day. The car owner took orders on behalf of the village and returned with the goods. Up to this point everything had been made in the village and exchanged by barter. But now it was possible to buy clothes and factory-made goods from shops in Siena. The social structure began to change, money was needed, and goods did not have to be made by hand. Around that same time the last cutting of the *ginestra* for making fabric occurred.

There was another revolution just over fifty years ago–the gramophone. Pari once boasted a band of musicians who played at weddings, dances and even provided the accompaniment to opera in the village square. A special occasion was the celebration of San Biagio (St. Blaise), the patron saint of the village. One year, representatives of the village made a trip to Grosseto–about 38km south of Pari–by a combination of bus and bullock cart and brought back a gramophone that was used to provide music for the San Biagio celebrations. Today there is radio and television but no village band.

The end of the 1950s also saw an economic revolution in central Italy. It was a period of industrialization, of the opening of factories and offices. It was a time when people left their villages to find work in the city. And so the wheat fields were sold off and houses were no longer inhabited. Over that period the population fell from around 1200 to the present number of just under 200. As we have seen, in the past people could live off the land with little need for cash. Today the land alone cannot support a family without additional income.

In the village there are masons who know the traditional methods of building with stone. Plumbers and electricians have work for months to come. But others must now work outside Pari in banks and offices, hotels and restaurants, drive buses or serve in bars on the highway. None of these jobs can be found within Pari itself. So what is the economic future of the village? How will it change? What work will the young people of Pari have when they grow up? Indeed will there be anything to keep them in the village? And Pari is only one of so many villages in rural Europe– and I imagine that a similar fate is faced by small communities in North America and much of the rest of the world. And once a village dies then so much history and knowledge dies with it. Each time an old person is buried in Pari something irreplaceable is lost in addition to a life. It may be knowledge of healing plants, a recipe, a story, a memory or even a particular dialect, modes of expression and old words no longer in common usage.

But despite all these changes the village remains closely knit. There is even a curious remnant of the barter system involving a network of small debts. On the first of each month we used to visit Rosita, the owner of the first house we rented in Pari. She would invite us in for a glass of *vin santo* and *cantucci*. But whenever I tried to raise the issue of paying her the month's rent she would say, "Come back tomorrow." On another occasion I had to be in London for several months and a neighbor, Paolo, renewed the insurance on my car. On returning to the village Paolo introduced me with, "This is my great friend, David, he owed me 600 euros for two months." In this way a subtle network of mutual obligations and favors is established, and serves as a cement to hold a community together.

Even trying to pay the bill at the local restaurants can be a major enterprise; when you ask for it you are generally told, "Come back tomorrow," or "Come back next week." I had become so used to this way of working that the following embarrassing event occurred. I was visiting the Vatican Observatory at Castel Gandolfo with two colleagues from Pari, Arnold and Shantena. After the meeting we went to dinner, ate well and then ordered ice creams. At the end of the meal we stood up and walked very leisurely out of the restaurant and across the piazza to where our car had been parked. It was only an hour later, while driving back to Pari that Arnold asked me, "Did you pay for the meal?" "No," I replied, "did you?" "No, I didn't pay," said Arnold. "Maybe Shantena paid." We had become so conditioned to paying for meals some days later that we had simply forgotten to ask for the bill.

As a theoretical physicist I had spent part of my life in an ivory tower but my contact with Native Americans and then the inhabitants of a medieval village had widened my horizons. Now I was beginning to think of the ethical implications of economics. It was clear that economic inequalities had a role to play in sowing the seeds of war and corruption. Studies have shown that with proper funding it would be possible to eradicate a number of diseases that ravage the Third World. If the money spent on cruise missiles could be pointed in another direction it would help to solve so many of the problems that face the developing world, and if the world changed in a radical way maybe we would not need all those weapons of defense and mass destruction. Economics is also tied to the international flow of information and the advance of science and technology. It is a key factor, for example, in the way scientists or engineers working in a developing country could gain access to the most up-to-date technical articles in their field.

I had never taken a particular interest in economics but now

I was questioning the impact that the small flow of money associated with the Pari Center had on the village. In turn I was finding that the Pari Center was being pulled into the grip of economics. The first hint of why we should have been taking notice came from Ed Nell, an economist visiting from the New School University in New York, who explained how fragile the economic world could be. In the early 1960s around three times more money was traded internationally than goods. Today it is vastly more. At the click of a mouse, enormous sums of money flash across the globe under no one's control. According to Nell this is a potentially unstable situation that could easily become chaotic. No one, from a peasant working in the fields of a developing country to the CEO of a multinational company, is insulated from the impact of global economics.

We had a visit from Ernesto Illy of Illycaffè. Illy was deeply interested in the ethical side of business and the economic tensions between the First and Third Worlds. Thanks to his encouragement, and that of the Monte dei Paschi di Siena bank, we ran an international conference entitled "Corporate Ethics, Globalization and Economic Instabilities."

The Pari Center has become a member of SPES the European Forum on Spirituality in Economic and Social Life and sent Shantena Sabbadini to the founding meeting. (At the inaugural meeting participants felt the term spirituality should not be confined to those of defined religious groups but to all: atheist, agnostic and believers alike who felt a sense of wonder and respect at the world.) We have also been discussing with Eric Weislogel of the Metanexus Institute ways of promoting the idea of a Global Academy. And during a visit, the author and environmentalist, Colin Tudge, suggested that Pari should become a "Network of Networks."

As time went on we created a network of people interested in the role of Ethics, Trust and Loyalty in the worlds of business and economics. Another Pari network is concerned with education. Inevitably as we also talked to economists at the University of Siena and the Monte dei Paschi di Siena bank we decided to join forces with EFA–a Siena-based association concerned with Ethics, Finance and Environment. This resulted, amongst other things in an international conference "Ethical Choices in Society, the Economy and the Environment."

At the end of the conference we invited speakers and several of the participants to Pari where they spent the morning talking to members of the village and listening to the problems the community faced. Following this we all met over lunch and continued talking until the early evening. It was clear that we wished to go beyond ideas and proposals towards something more practical. In this way the Pari Network was born. It is intended to be both a hotbed for new ideas and a catalyst for projects and activities. The network can be accessed at www.parinetwork.org.

The Center itself is registered in Italy as a non-profit association and has now (Fall 2006) been running for over six years during which time quite a few changes have occurred. There is now a village library in one of the rooms of the *palazzo*. Another room has been converted into a children's play center run by our daughter, Eleanor, with such activities as dance, exercise, art, crafts, music, theater and even cooking. There is also talk of restoring the upper floor of the *palazzo*, which contains a large room that could be used for concerts, dance, theater or lectures to large groups.

Keeping the Center going on a daily basis takes a great deal of time and hard work–even the business of replying to e-mail enquiries each day can take a few hours. I'm afraid we do not have the mindset to run it like an efficient business; in fact, as one visitor remarked, the whole thing is more like a work of art. It's always a matter of seeing what fits, or what is out of balance, or what needs to be added where. In this way our actions and decisions are more aesthetic than economic.

Another of our activities is that of recording local history. Following one of our conferences, several participants decided they would like to give a gift to the Center. They asked what we would like. I replied, "A digital video camera." We have since used the camera to make records of local festivals and events as well as recording talks and conferences. We also began to tape interviews with the surviving members of the village band. Several of these interviews have now been edited and some short clips placed on the Pari Center Web site. I well remember during one interview that Remo, he of the birdcalls, sang a song he had composed to sing outside his wife's window. She had left him for a man with a better suit, he told us, and so he serenaded her until she finally returned to him. As he sang to us and remembered his dead wife, tears came into his eyes. We are continuing with these interviews and plan to include the way cloth was made from *ginestra*, the stories of those who died or went missing during World War II and interviews with some of the young people about their ideas for the future of the village.

Earlier in this chapter I wrote of the importance of education in developing countries. This has been a constant refrain in many of our discussions in Pari. One who responded in a practical way has been Roy McWeeny who, along with several friends, is developing a series of workbooks that can be downloaded without charge from the Pari Center Web site. At present twenty such books are planned and these will provide a complete course of self-study in mathematics and the sciences. With funding these books will also be available in Arabic, Spanish, French and other languages. We have even been thinking of a Web site where students can go for help.

I too had books to write, for the Pari Center has been only one part of my life. But, as with art and music, the business of publishing also has its fashions. Some topics are "in," others are "out." At the moment the sort of books I write seem to be "out." I learned this when my excellent editor of four earlier books explained to me that "books of ideas" were no longer selling that well; publishers were looking for science as a detective story, or science that could be hung on some sort of a hook. This confirmed my worst fears, since I had already noticed that the titles of science books had begun to change; now it was all *Newton's Nostril*, *Faraday's Left Foot*, or *The Story of Sludge* and *The Search for…*–whatever, just add in a noun and you have your next book. And I am not joking here. Once a colleague and I were approached by an editor to write a book provided that the word "SEVEN" was included in its title!

This news about publishing was unfortunate but not demoralizing because I can never forget the lesson of Robert M. Pirsig's *Zen and the Art of Motorcycle Maintenance*. One summer the physicist, David Finkelstein, was a visitor at the National Research Council in Ottawa. He brought with him a manuscript that he had been asked by a publisher to review for possible publication. David liked the book and told me he was going to write something very favorable. A few years later the book was published to considerable success but I also learned that it had first been rejected by most of New York's main publishers.

That was the same year my agent made appointments for me in New York to meet some leading editors. I explained to one of them that I wanted to write a book on synchronicity and was asked, "But why not write a book like *Zen and the Art of Motorcycle Maintenance*?" To this I replied, "But didn't your publishing house reject Pirsig's manuscript?" Reluctantly she agreed that they had. A few years later, I was asked if I could write a book, "Just like the one on Prozac." Hence my cynicism about literary fashion. Maybe it's not so much driven by what the public wants as the result of desperate attempts by bewildered editors and publishing houses to give the public what they think it wants.

I discussed the state of publishing with several of my contemporaries who told me they had left the leading houses because they felt they no longer served their best interests; they were now going to small presses. I also talked to David Godwin, my agent in London. David confirmed that the face of publishing was indeed changing. In part he felt it was caused by the large chains of booksellers who charge a publisher a fee for placing a book in a window and a fee to display on a table. According to the London Observer at Christmas time 2005, Waterstone's, the large British chain of bookstores, were demanding 65-70 percent discount on all titles. In addition, they were asking for contributions of £30,000 ($52,000) or more towards marketing costs for each promoted book. As a result, choice was being restricted–larger and larger piles of fewer and fewer books. Godwin said that he was trying to resist that trend and encouraged me to think about alternative publishing possibilities.

In this way the notion of Pari Publishing was born. Why did we ourselves not publish the sorts of books that we felt were serious, important or represented an alternative point of view? After all, with the advent of the CD revolution many musicians had created their own small, independent labels, why not do the same with books? In this we were encouraged by the novelist, Alison MacLeod, who came up with some interesting suggestions. As so my wife and daughter registered Pari Publishing as a legal entity in Italy.

And their first book? It is the one you are reading now. It has been designed by my son-in-law Andrea Barbieri and the company now have a number of other books in the works. As to the origin of the particular book you are now holding in your hand, it evolved out of an invitation by Santi di Renzo, the owner of an Italian publishing company who was bringing out a series of short autobiographies in Italian written by well-known scientists and thinkers. Would I write one for his series? I did this but reserved the English rights. When the idea of Pari Publishing was born, I began to think: why not expand that book and make it our inaugural volume? And here it is. You are reading it now. You are in at the birth. Thank you for buying it, or borrowing it from a friend or the public library.

I have more or less come to the end of the story; at least for now. I began this journey by looking through a microscope and by gazing at pictures as my aunt turned the pages of a book. I thought about the problem of evil and my aunt explained Plato's notion of government. I chose science as a vocation, and for many years thought hard about the nature of matter. I met David Bohm. I sat in a tepee and talked to Native American elders. I visited artists' studios and am still planning collaborative endeavors with some of them. Creative people in a variety of organizations have supported my endeavors, often simply because they liked the ideas. I came as a stranger to the village of Pari and was openly and warmly received. Our plans to create a cultural center met with total cooperation. In turn, I have now begun to think of such things as ethics, gentle action and the future of the world. We are embarking on a publishing venture. Most of the good things that occurred in my life were freely given to me through the generosity of others.

Thank you all again.

F. David Peat

www.fdavidpeat.com
www.paricenter.com
www.parinetwork.org

Pari Publishing is an independent publishing company, based in a medieval Italian village. Our books appeal to a broad readership and focus on innovative ideas and approaches from new and established authors who are experts in their fields. We publish books in the areas of science, society, psychology, and the arts.

Our books are available at all good bookstores or online at
www.paripublishing.com

If you would like to add your name to our email list to receive information about our forthcoming titles and our online newsletter please contact us at **newsletter@paripublishing.com**

Visit us at **www.paripublishing.com**

Pari Publishing Sas
Via Tozzi, 7
58040 Pari (GR)
Italy

Email: info@paripublishing.com